DON'T

DON'T

THE

ESSENTIAL GUIDE

TO

PUBLICITY

IN

NEW YORK CITY

&

ANY OTHER CITY THAT MATTERS

MARCO LARSEN

FOREWORD

I love New York City.

Without question, we live in the capital of the world—the city is simply effervescent. Even as a kid visiting family here, I can remember always wanting to be a part of the fervor—in fact I was jealous of it. Painfully so.

So when I moved here from Denver, Colorado I was motivated with equal energy to feel like I belonged—which can take years, or never happen at all. Publicity being my profession, it was the perfect time in my career to endure NYC's unique "sink or swim" schooling that finely tunes the PR expert.

I went to parties, put on events, cavorted in the Bowery, and took in as much as I could (many times to the detriment of my liver). And in all of this, I learned that distinction is not merited through inaction, or by being passive. That doing "the work" is essential for developing character—which is, and always will be, the desired currency for New York City.

Publicity is a rich and dynamic profession. For young aspirants, there is no rulebook to date that can walk you through treacherous professional territory or be at your side before you make that very awkward gaffe. Save, of course, this book.

Now of publicists: I don't like them. The emboldened commentary within is a reflection of the many types I abhor, and the others I uphold as perfect illustrations. With relish, I verbally assail "handbag publicists" and with no lack of appetite do the same for lackey-like company drones. But please bear in mind that in the beginning stages of a career (where you may be right now) I did exactly what I rail against within, with equal... well... enthusiasm.

Please enjoy DON'T—and by all means, learn from it.

– Marco Larsen

CONTENTS

INTRODUCTION

The Breed Standard (in New York City),
by *Carson Kressley*

To succeed in the world of media, no matter what coast you're on, you have to know the rules of the game. If you're playing in New York—well done. I love people with gumption.

You've heard what everyone says about New York: it's a tough town. But no one moves here for an easy ride. New York appreciates nothing more than quality, and here it's everywhere. Everyone's beautiful, everyone's got dash, and all of them are here for something. Anything. Everything!

I know a lot about making it in this town. The people who succeed at the game in New York are the ones who figure out the rules and have the creativity and determination to make those rules work for them.

I've been riding and showing horses for most of my life. It's a passion of mine, and a world my family's been involved in since before Carson was a Kressley. When I decided to move from Allentown, Pennsylvania to New York City it was not a surprise to me or my parents, maybe because of a choice that I'd made when I was fifteen years old: to show American Saddlebred horses.

My grandparents had always bred show ponies, and I loved them, but at every show we would go to I couldn't keep my eyes off the Saddlebreds. I mean, just listen to how the United States Equestrian Federation describes the breed:

"The American Saddlebred is the epitome of the show horse. He carries himself with an attitude that eludes description— some call it 'class', presence, quality, style or charm. This superior air distinguishes his every movement." I aspired to nothing less.

And it wasn't just the attitude of the horses but the nature of showing Saddlebreds that drew me to the sport. Riders of Saddlebreds are as much on display as their horses. In shows riders are judged on ease and control; to excel a rider must "show himself to the best advantage."

Mastering the required dress code was the easy part (surprise!) In order to succeed as a rider I first needed to master the tangled web of rules, restrictions and customs that dominate Saddlebred shows. What separates a good rider from a prize winning one, though, is an ability to be so comfortable with the show ring regulations that his or her natural personality can shine through. Just as the Equestrian Federation tries to describe the American Saddlebred as defined by "class", it's that certain intangible something that defines excellence.

Since New York has always demanded excellence, that's what you've got to figure out how to provide. The challenge, the excitement, and the sheer quality of New York City drew me. Once here, I knew I had two missions: figure out the rules, and then figure out how to make them work for me.

I'm still working through this process with new projects I take on, and even in the horse show world. In 2008 I rode to a 2nd place finish at the World Championship Horse Show in Louisville, Kentucky, in between taping seasons of *How to Look Good Naked*. And that's not the end. Not for any of my careers, riding or otherwise.

So, onward and upward ladies and gentlemen! You've got the rules of the game in your hand—make them yours. Learn how to show yourself to your best advantage, so that people will find themselves unable to describe your presence fully; call it class, quality, style, or charm, no matter the word, let that be you.

JHONNY CROCODILE – FRUMPY

FIRST SUIT GUY – TIGHT FITTER

HIPSTER – ALL BOOBS

CHAPTER ONE

FIRST
IMPRESSIONS

Variations in dress, style and carriage are infinite – and infinitely subjective. Do you take the time to consider those you find attractive? Off-putting? Perhaps even those so lackluster they leave little impression at all?

New York is the capital of accomplishment, the dress code and marketing politics more exacting here than any place in the world. It is a feat to make a name here in any discipline: finance, art, publishing, sports, fashion, cuisine or celebrity. Manhattan might lag in cornering the banal, but plenty of other places vie quite well for that achievement, and—with apologies to the hinterland, I'm sure—they are not where you've chosen to be.

As a newcomer to our industry in a city that expects perfection your task will be a daunting one. Editors, producers, writers and marketing executives have been here for years, and certainly get up earlier than you in more than one regard. Appealing to their better sides will take serious effort on your part. For a lucky few, this process is intuitive, second nature; hungry, already ahead of the game, their success is pre-determined. The rest will need tools to navigate even the most carnivorous environments with confidence. You'll find this book one such tool.

That your appearance, demeanor and expertise be up-to-snuff is fundamental to a winning first impression. Everyone you meet will pin you with a mental resume. Poise and polish lend you credibility and encourage a more open reception from your audience. The faintest faux pas, critiqued by our pundit elite even unwittingly, can cause your best intentions to come crashing down before you even open your freshman mouth.

Keeping fit and well-maintained enhances all aspects of your life. Mentally you are more confident and alert; physically you are more attractive. Advantageous in any profession, these traits are absolute requisites in publicity—industries fuelled by *image* and dominated by the pacesetters that best decode, construct and project it.

I will avoid harshness where fitness is concerned, knowing this is a delicate subject, and that we want to get off to a good start. Being slim is never mandatory. Being persuasive is. Shape and size are one thing, aplomb quite another. Nonetheless, absolute *attractiveness* is what we strive for. The benefits of a winning, healthy *appearance* are more consequential than you might care to believe. So do with that what you will. The first few points in this chapter will tend to focus on men's comportment and attire, the last few exclusively on women's, for whom the rules are more fluid and complex. Whatever your stripe, you'd be wise to consider both.

Now, then, ladies and gentlemen:

DON'T FORGET TO COMB YOUR HAIR!

...or to shave, gentlemen. ...or to put on your face, ladies. An unkempt mane (unless you're wildly beautiful and under 21), poorly maintained skin, brows, nails, nose hair or pungent odors detract from any performance. Don't fight an uphill battle. Maintain an immaculate standard, and your audience will be inclined to hear your words rather than wonder why they should listen to you at all.

Here's a simple example.
At an interview with a national publication, one of the firms with which I work had their PR assistant sit in on the proceedings. As the conversation progressed I found myself increasingly riveted by a dark scruff shadowing the underside of the young man's mouth. Indeed, it proved to be a rather obvious patch of stubble he had somehow missed in his morning toilette.

A trifling flaw? Arguably. Yet it drew me inexorably into a withering inventory of everything else I could critique about him. Once those renegade whiskers caught my eye I couldn't ignore how generally unkempt he looked: pallid, poorly dressed, his slapdash grooming an invitation to evaluate his entire appearance—and presentation—negatively.

Subsequent discussions didn't bear much fruit for the inelegant gentleman. His thoughts met with little interest, slight surprise, and I could only imagine his interlocutors, rather than listening to what he had to say, lost in distraction: "What the hell is that on his face? Did he not see that this morning? Ah, well, he must be too overwhelmed, or too oblivious, to correct it." Even such charitable conclusions were probably not the mark he had looked to make.

In any business setting at all, really, it is only proper to look well groomed. Wake up with a shower! Shine some light on your face and spruce it up. Try some deodorant, a light fragrance, and some toothpaste before you go.

Now, doesn't that feel better?

DON'T
DRESS LIKE YOU JUST
FLEW IN FROM LOS
ANGELES.

I never fail to notice the impression neophyte marketers from the West Coast make, their blasé manner underscored by what, in the People's Republic of L.A., passes for a business wardrobe. By all means, when in SoCal do as the Angelenos do. When in New York, please just don't embarrass us all on your behalf! This also goes for Tokyo, London, or any other city that distinguishes between dressing for business and dressing for the cover of *Hello*.

Another poignant example:
At a series of recent press meetings, I watched a gentleman pitch his line of skin care, which shall remain nameless. A denizen of L.A., he had an easy, wispy way about him that was genuinely charming; unfortunately, he also wore what looked like his only black suit with a bright red, open shirt... (excruciating pause)... Must I go on?

In the end, there were hugs all round, the editors lovingly assured him of success (in stores, just not in their magazines), and he left ebullient.

He never received a shred of editorial.

Casting a seasoned, gimlet eye on an endless parade of luxuries, editors are paid to judge. *Almost* doesn't cut it. The competition's too fierce, the coveted media space too scarce. In a cherry-pick of the pop cultural profusion, editors seek out *overall* effect: Product, Packaging, Persona. Drop one ball and you drop them all. Would you wear a gorgeous fragrance decanted from an unsightly bottle? If the quintessentially chic Chanel No. 5 were poured into a glitzy flacon with Paris Hilton as spokesmodel, would it even *be* Chanel No. 5 anymore?

As it turns out, the editors' unspoken verdict was spot on: our boy never made his collection a success.

Don't get me wrong. Talent and charisma will be a tremendous asset. But in NYC, you must be informed, dedicated, straightforward *and* perfectly dressed. Don't just observe the rules— perfect the details.

DON'T
SLOB OUT AT HAPPY
HOUR.

Men, nothing makes you look like a part time businessman and full time troglodyte like purposely disarranging the day's carefully perfected panoply the minute you're off the clock. I'm well aware that many an exuberant young buck is keen to doff the collar promptly at 5 pm, loosen the old tie and head down to the pub (a foray, incidentally, for which Wall Street was originally set aside). But how does your after hours deportment reflect on your character during the day?

Any *sober* evening visit to South Street Seaport or the Financial District's more raucous establishments will confirm the social template that one should elegantly avoid personifying. Unfairly or not, you'll find (if you're lucky enough to become aware of it) that once you've evoked this stereotype, it sticks: you and the lads bellowing into your pitchers of Silver Bullet about football, the betting spreads, which chicks you banged while your girlfriend was away, and occasionally staggering off to moisten the washroom floor.

If this does indeed sum up your brain trust and the way you wish your colleagues to perceive you, then fine. Pop that collar when the whistle blows, belt out a Yabba-dabba-doo, and bolt for the elevators.

But hey! It's been a long day, and this business can be stressful. Why *not* cut loose a little with the guys? Only trust me on one thing. Even those unregenerate savages, your best friends, will learn to respect you further and take you more seriously when they see you paying attention to every detail of your career development, including the image you project about town. They may pretend they don't; they may even have a few choice descriptions to apply; but inwardly they'll wish they had your discipline. Beer and Jaeger? Who could resist! Just order your shots with aplomb.

And do watch your step on that washroom floor.

DON'T
FALL PREY TO THE
CASUAL CONUNDRUM.

Styling, gentlemen, is very much about propriety. Jeans, designer t-shirts, boots, and jewelry other than watches, cufflinks, and wedding bands read as juvenile. Aside from celebrity hairdressers, those who make a living playing the guitar, and anyone who's joined the circus, takes daily anti-psychotics or designs denim, this rule brooks no exception. Also note: women worth sleeping with do not find "cute" socks alluring.

(This rule, incidentally, may equally be applied to your underwear.)

Rather, the elegant gentleman fashions his dress on a fine British gin after the hunt: give it a moment. Classic style, fit and fabric don't overwhelm, yet they impress more powerfully than razzamatazz. Rest assured that editors, who hold the keys to your success, appreciate the professionalism behind a well turned-out ensemble, and quite the reverse when you show up looking casual and trendy.

DON'T
TAKE CHANCES UNTIL
YOU'RE ON TOP OF
YOUR GAME.

You may be tempted to give in early on, dressing down from time to time with familiar clientele. Don't. Respect is earned; start by dressing consistently with distinction.

For gentlemen it is best to err on the conservative side (not George Bush conservative; Chester Barrie conservative—and no, I'm not telling you who that is. Look it up!) Until your own style develops sufficiently, flattering *both* your person and your personality, observe the following.

DON'T WEAR BAD SUITS. Slightly fitted and hanging gracefully at mid-section, a classic, well-cut suit shows discrimination. Until you can afford a $2500+, true "bespoke suit", tailors—not hacks masquerading in some dry cleaners—can fit those you've bought off-the-rack to great effect.

DON'T NEGLECT THE COLLAR. "Spread" collars are generally best: for the bold, a "cut away"; for the tall, a longer one (avoid the Gotti-esque). A Gingham pattern or cotton herring-bone lends European panache; accents and tie vary the persona.

DON'T WEAR BUTTONED CUFFS. With any jacket, wear double cuffs (as Americans call "French cuffs"). Cuff links without a jacket? Mumbai nightclub. Buttoned cuffs (or collar) with a jacket? Lazy!

DON'T OVERDO THE TIE. Ties can add dash—or bad taste. Solid colors look great; with a black suit whatever pops, except multiple prints. Modern preppy works as well, cross patterns and checks, but please, go to the Madison Avenue Ralph Lauren store to figure this out—don't assume.

DON'T CARRY A BACKPACK. ...or a briefcase. The first is sophomoric, the second, well, square. Lawyer bags, opening from the top, are handy. Black, brown, tan, anything leather with an aged (not beat up) "patina" works. Aim for quality and understatement.

DON'T UNBUTTON YOUR JACKET. It's insipid. Most of the people you see doing this have preternaturally large guts that they would do better to keep covered. Keep it tight. Keep it in. Button your suit coat.

DON'T DEBASE YOUR FEET. Shoes demarcate style and good taste. Women always (always) gauge a man's sophistication by his shoes. Get it? Avoid anything cheap, uncomfortable, or overly trendy; design should suggest craftsmanship and classic elegance. That's all. Opt for an English- or Italian-made black Oxford, wingtip. Logos, tassels, fancy folderol: Don't! It's a liability.

D O N ' T
C O M M U T E   I N   R U N N I N G
S H O E S .

Ladies! Remember Melanie Griffith in *Working Girl?* Right. Maybe, like her, you really are schlepping hours a day between your gig in Manhattan and your crash pad in the outer boroughs—but why advertise it?

A killer image is only killer if applied at all times. Women at the executive level, to which I trust you aspire, are either driven home, take a taxi, or endure a brief subway ride—in their *heels*. Putting on trainers signals that the life you envision is one of assisting someone in their shoes— not filling those shoes yourself.

...and, of course, that you have poor taste.

Looking like a million dollars as you saunter between office and street shows that you are always "on". You may not receive daily congratulations for staying sharp, but believe me, you'll leave far fewer eyes rolling in your wake. Additionally, coming and going on a high note boosts your own confidence and sense of career purpose no matter what your position may currently be. As for comfort and convenience on the Staten Island Ferry: why not just commute in your robe and curlers? You look about as distinguished wearing tennies with a business ensemble.

Not to endorse inequity, but the fact is that, in business as everywhere else, women are ranked for appearance more than men. Uncomfortable though you may find them, the aptly named 'power' heels impart an authoritative air to a woman's office attire.

That said, women are not *utterly* restricted to stilettos for a proper look. While the polished professional wears chic shoes in as well as to and from the office and saves tennis shoes for tennis, a lower heel, refined summer wedge, or elegant flat is also appropriate. It's just not quite as sharp.

Speaking of sharp, the following offers a few more pointers on the desirable wardrobe.

DON'T
OVERSPICE.

Too hip, too cute, too edgy, excessive fashions communicate professional naiveté. That trendy item all the chicks want to rock; every extremity decked with bling; the extra inch or three of scenic décolletage—these are all blatant tags of immaturity.

Look: there's obviously nothing quite like flaunting it while you're young. If you do have a fantastic figure, wrap it proudly in Diane von Furstenberg—and *go out for cocktails.*

Meanwhile, back at the *office* your position depends on *power,* and power, it must be emphasized, goes far beyond inspiring men to clownish behavior. Strong women climb the ladder by displaying stellar talent. Stellar accomplishments. Stellar execution ... not just a stellar derrière.

Head to toe in one designer? *Interdit!* (It's French. Look it up.) Flashy logos announcing your status? Regrettable.

Advertising only a woman's insecurity, inelegance, and lack of individualism, showy, logo-driven ensembles are the sartorial equivalent of discussing how rich you are. In contrast, the modern, classic style of the *dame distinguée,* centered on flattering cuts, well-chosen fabrics and deft accessorizing, reflects her enviable taste in all matters. My friend Carlota Espinosa, consummate fashionista and former FOX producer, shares the following:

DON'T WEAR A SUIT! Not in interviews, not at meetings. It says you don't understand those you'll be working with. Rather, wear a simple dress with a thin belt, or trousers and a feminine but not frilly blouse.

DON'T WEAR NUDE PANTYHOSE. Ever! Wear black tights if you must. Nicks? Bruises? Unsightliness? It happens. Wear pants.

DON'T FOLLOW TRENDS. Who wants to be seen with the same "must-have" purse as every other silly young thing?

DON'T WEAR FLIP-FLOPS, for goodness' sake! There are plenty of stylish flats you can wear instead.

DON'T EVEN BOTHER WITH A MID-HEEL, square-toed loafer in black calf. Nobody—*nobody*—wants to see it. Ever.

DON'T SKIMP. Treat yourself to delicious shoes. Have them resoled every four weeks or so. And no, dear, champagne does not come out of satin. Get a backup pair!

CHAPTER TWO

TACTICS
AND
STRATEGY

Consider the great media stories of the last fifty years, those that marked cultural turning points or defined a year, a decade, even a generation. What immediately stands out to anyone in our profession is how often these stories portrayed a consumer trend, a celebrity, a product or a brand. Apple alone accounts for a substantial share; the Beatles even more, &c., &c.

We live in a culture which imagines itself in large part by what and how it consumes. The media is the prism through which these images are formed. As the publicist, you don't just stand at its source; you yourself could well be that source.

First, however, you must know what it is that you want people to see and, second, what will ignite their interest. Getting it right can make you the next media rockstar—getting it wrong, the next intern who *almost* hit the mark.

You know the people who write, edit and produce the stories. Regional and demographic intelligence is crucial, too: *effective* publicity requires a broad understanding of the public poised to consume these stories. A detailed awareness of *who* they are, *how* they live, and *where*. Above all else, however, you must understand the client whom you wish to place into the story. A winning strategy aces the trifecta: Media, Market, Message.

Clients often don't know what's best for them. That's why they retain you.

Knowing the particularities of a diverse media market demands instinct and intelligence. Understanding your client does, too. Relying solely on their established marketing position will not suffice. Marketing collateral doesn't contain enough substance—or candor—to be informative to you, much less the media; your flimsy story will swiftly be exposed. Messages conveying image alone amount to mere advertising.

Publicity establishes credibility. It is the only arrow in the marketing quiver that has the ability to create a third-party endorsement—essential for selling any product or service.

Knowing your clients means knowing who and where their customers are, what those customers prefer, what in their world interests them and how they learn of it. It means knowing the history of the product or service your client provides, the processes and conditions that make it possible.

And it means knowing the competitors who vie with your client to provide that product or service. What marketplace position does each side occupy? What motivates them? What is it that sets each apart?

While advertising and publicity are distinct, your client can afford to neglect neither. In fact, the two may cross multiply in fruitful ways, as when ads become media stories in their own right.

Nor does basing stories on fact mean banishing creativity. Preciosity makes a frivolous impression; it's true, but you'll always win editorial placements that fulfill marketing needs by finding angles that offer information as well as élan.

How can you imbue your stories with both? Read on.

DON'T CONFUSE PUBLICITY WITH MARKETING.

Good news! Your client comes referred by an ad agency with a complete marketing plan that comprises a slick press kit, a series of broadcast spots in the can and a sweeping print strategy. All you have to do is start calling newspapers, get a few TV interviews and maybe whip up a couple of cool events. Your job couldn't get any easier, right?

Not necessarily.

People who think they understand the value of publicity may treat it as merely another appendage of advertising or marketing. In fact, the two are completely distinct; even with an already-existing marketing or advertising strategy, publicity requires a separate, yet parallel, strategy altogether.

So your client has a renowned agency with a brilliant campaign already in place. So their sales have jumped X percent since their series of media spots started running in target markets. How does this help you? Well, maybe it gives you a bubblier client to work with, but beyond that, not much. Appearing in an ad means simply that you have enough money to gain access to a certain club (*Vogue, Forbes,* &c.) to court customers.

Successful publicity, by contrast, means that the club has chosen you. This perceived third-party endorsement makes all the difference. It's earned media. It's nine out of ten "dentists" recommending your client's product in an ad versus one beloved national TV host hanging on your client's every word *between* the ads.

As different as the effects of these two approaches are, so too are the strategies that make each one successful. To be eye-catching, even outrageous, to convey an emotion or capture a mood is often all an ad needs to succeed in energizing the consumer to rise, go forth and buy stuff. A media placement, on the other hand, must provide information of such intrinsic value that the consumer not only *a)* becomes aware of the brand but *b)* personally identifies with it and *c)* accepts it as quintessential.

It is media based on informed persuasion, not dollars.

DON'T IMAGINE ONE SIZE FITS ALL.

There's something poignantly awkward about watching the members of a quietly self-contained community gamely attempt to digest a message that implicitly overlooks their very existence. Putting a national resort developer on to talk about $50,000-a-year fractional ownership plans in a market where that figure outstrips the median income, for example, is probably not the best route to a warm reception.

The developer may even be building within the market in question, and the story might in fact serve your client well in national syndication. But if it's only playing to the potential staff of the resort rather than its potential patrons, you might as well head down to Florida and try to talk snow tires.

It's not that your client's project has no relevance to the community. In fact, it's most likely vital. But in attempting to cram a national story down local outlets' throats, you've overlooked what's relevant about it to their specific market: not the gorgeous private residences their viewers can't afford, but the business, employment opportunities and day-guest amenities that could truly excite them.

Most likely, however, you needn't worry. This story will never make it to air in the first place, because local broadcasters simply won't return your calls. Instead, you need to approach them with something relevant. Call or write with concrete reasons why their audience will be interested in your client. In arriving at these angles, the questions you ask will be the same for national as for local media, but the answers will necessarily be different:

> How many people in the target market are directly affected by your client—and how? Is your client's industry growing? Where is the potential for more? Can your client be tied to relevant trends or current events in the target market? Most importantly: why *would* people care?

Once you can answer those questions to your own satisfaction, you're ready for WPIX Morning News.

DON'T BRING A GRENADE TO THE ARCHERY RANGE.

Obviously, the foregoing works conversely, as well. Your work on behalf of the Hungarian Puli Association's new breed standard, for example, will probably reach its target audience more effectively in *American Kennel Gazette* than it will on *Good Morning, America*. How much does the average stiff care about the judging points for brushed versus corded coats?

This is not to say that it's necessarily hard to place yet another story about an exotic-looking pet breed. Just that a story of local, or otherwise specifically defined, interest only gets diluted by the national outlets' imperative to make it resonate with the widest share of their audience.

Not only will a story that's going out to tens of millions of people be stripped of anything detailed or resonant, the specific audience you most want to reach are too widely scattered among those tens of millions. To blunt your story's edge still further, any random dog-fanciers who do run across it will take less interest. It will appear addressed not to the edification of breed sophisticates like themselves but to the idle amusement of plebes who can't tell a Mittelschnauzer from a mutt.

Even if you do decide to go national, you'll receive more bandwidth and thus stronger, more focused attention by channeling your story into a single, major network or big-market news source than by trying to blanket the dial. National media place great emphasis on exclusive coverage, and your pitch needs to fit the outlet's audience base. Anything that's generic or running elsewhere goes to the bottom of the lineup, is relegated to a small patch of an inside page, or discarded altogether, simply as it creates less differentiation from the rest of what's out there. Individual media outlets aim to define themselves as *ahead* of a trend, or *first* with a story—not as one of many, simultaneously spotlighting the same information.

Be specific when you need to (trade publications, specialty television shows, &c.), and bring out the big guns when you've got the biggest targets to hit.

DON'T
LOSE TOUCH WITH
CURRENT EVENTS.

In case you hadn't noticed, you're working with the media now, if not actually within it. There's no other crowd more intensely concerned with appearing *au courant*, if not avant-garde. For you to sit there in the midst of a conversation staring blankly in response to a casual reference that everyone else takes as common knowledge will not do.

So put down the joystick and the bong, and pick up your remote, a mouse or the newspaper. Start figuring out what's been going on these past couple decades. You're going to need it.

Whether the conversation turns to fashion, sport, arts, travel, entertainment, politics or global affairs your facility not just in keeping up but in contributing will be taken as a measure of your general acumen by those you most need to impress. Being in the know implicitly identifies you as a source of intelligence that others can turn to their own advantage. It makes you a prize contact rather than just another in the daily procession of supplicants showing up with their hands out.

You will also need to enhance your cultural literacy. By sharing a common vocabulary with those to whose company you aspire, you gain a quiet respect which may in turn grant you an entrée. We will explore this later, but take heed; turn off the TV and go to the opera (or any number of other enlightening options), lest you become known more for the breadth of your *Two and a Half Men* trivia.

Furthermore, being familiar with the trends and events going on all around you will powerfully facilitate your core job of crafting varied, original, timely story ideas that resonate with ever-shifting audiences. Actually comprehending the cutting edge in your clients' fields, for example, helps you position them more strategically against the backdrop of their industries.

Similarly, an awareness of local events in a market you wish to reach will help far more than all the focus groups in the world to transform your client's nationally calibrated message into one that's tailored to what's happening within the immediate community.

Knowing what's happening in the world affords countless relevant story angles and the ability to sense what makes a story tick – and when it's getting stale.

It also prevents your looking like an idiot over drinks.

DON'T BELIEVE THE CUSTOMER IS ALWAYS RIGHT.

They are far too often disastrously wrong. They don't know how the media operates; they don't understand the perspectives of particular outlets and editors; they don't know what will *interest* the audience rather than momentarily distract and possibly *annoy* them. They don't know how to appear poised and confident in the limelight. Indeed, half the time they don't even know how to dress for an interview.

They need you more than you realize.

Perhaps the worst fate that can befall your relationship with your client is for you to end up as a second marketing department. It is also one of the easiest. The client has a stack of market research and some really, really neat focus group metrics to push at you; a goofy ad reel that hauls in the phone calls; and a snazzy song-and-dance routine that's already worked wonders with investors and the bank.

(smirk)

This is publicity, not marketing. The intended result is greater audience familiarity and trust for your clients' brand, not just an immediate jump in sales (though that's good, too). It's absolutely crucial for your clients' long-term success that you shape a strategy to garner the most attention from the most reputable media sources. That you address your clients' market while retaining the firmest possible control over how they are presented. None of this has to do with peddling widgets.

Rather, it is a matter of cultivating both media and client so that the former will see the latter as a trusted source of reliable information about a particular realm of endeavor. It means knowing which outlets are both best positioned to reach the audience suited to your clients' product or service and most likely to reach quick simpatico with their personal and business character.

And it means talking your client out of that psychedelic, hand-painted necktie one more time.

DON'T
FORGET YOUR EDITING
HAT.

It demands a Pulitzer, by God! From the exhaustive research you zealously compiled right down to the perfectly polished prose, you've produced a masterpiece of substance and style. Of course, it's already 4,000 words and is still just a pitch, not a story, but what of that?

When you've worked hard fleshing out an idea that's particularly compelling to you, it can be difficult to remember that you yourself are not the story's writer, only its source—that your name ideally should never even come up in connection with it at all. This is all the more difficult if the story promises to serve your client's needs especially well.

Nonetheless, make sure you remember it.

Of course, once you're crammed full of information you should feel comfortable letting your creativity go. Brainstorm; pursue angles that might seem like dead ends; play with the idea. Passionate diligence can certainly make the difference between a piece that is merely placed in a routine publicity slot and one that editors or producers really warm to.

Brilliant ideas are one thing, the ability to convey them brilliantly quite another. At its core, publicity is communication; you must be able to hone inspiration into a concise, persuasive argument. Too many frills and furbelows just end up seeming frivolous; readers can't find the cake for the frosting. Moreover, all that superfluous blather is sure to be edited out once the story gets into the hands of the media. Professional writers are just going to fashion it into something succinct they can release to their audience.

It's not your job to cheerlead for a story. The days of pushing finished copy into wholesale publication ended decades ago. It is ultimately the journalist who fashions words and content into stories that the reader will enjoy. Your job is simply to set them down that path by furnishing them with perfect ideas and relevant facts.

DON'T
WRITE LIKE A P.R.
INTERN.

Please examine this specimen. And take warning: ###FOR IMMEDIATE RELEASE###

____wants you to join us for: Champagne and Shoes! [*Nice punctuation! Vividly captures the infantile, sinusoidal shriek that undoubtedly communicates your think-by-the-numbers condescension in person.*]

The ladies [LADIES! *Who invited Jerry Lewis?*] from____Shoes will be there to help you ring in the New Year with a bottle of bubbly [*meaning* champagne! *That's French!*] along with the freshest and trendiest resort styles!!! [*Nothing spells "style" like multiple exclamation points!!!*] While it's still brrrrr outside, toss your puffy jacket aside [*wouldn't be caught dead in a ditch in one, thanks*] and check out the latest sandals and espadrilles for that trip to Cabo you've been secretly planning...(shhh!) [*ugh*]

We'll see you at Bendel's 5th floor shoe salon on Saturday, January 6th to indulge in some chocolate covered strawberries, cupcakes, and truffles [*Is this for the shoes or the pig-out?*] before you buckle down and drag yourself to the gym.

[Fat f— —ing chance.] (Maybe we'll actually keep that resolution this year? Wink, wink.) *[ibid.]*

We'll be kicking it off *[Get it! Kicking? Shoes? Haaaaaaaaaaaa!]* at 2pm but no res necessary —we know you can't resist! *[Haaaaaaaaaaaaa!]* Any styles needed for photo/editorial can be taken with or sent via *[or taken via or sent with; or sent/taken via/with]* messenger later in the afternoon. Call Melissa at the showroom for any additional details, and get your FABULOUS selves *[BIG, fat asses]* down here!!! *[Painful...]*

Somebody needs immediate release, alright— from any job requiring sophistication, syntax or a clue. Oh, I'm being vicious? Indeed. Some-one placed this masterwork on the wire ser-vices and charged their trusting client *tall dollars* for the, ahem, publicity.

Eschew glib, tired phrases and concepts, old news and sophomoric flights of hyperbole: craft messages that are timely or timeless. Write like a grown up—not Tinky-Winky on Adderall.

DON'T
PEDDLE CANNED
GOODS.

In days of yore, publicists used video news releases (VNRs) to drum up journalistic interest. Essentially a packaged news segment all ready to air, these microwaveable niblets of journalism served two needs: those of publicists who didn't care how blatantly fake their story placements looked when they hit the screen, and those of journalists who had better things to do than, well, journalism.

As those halcyon days fade into obscurity, VNRs are met with increasing resistance from members of the media as audiences flee the dial in droves for content they actually trust. Yes, I mean the Internet, but nobody said there was any logic to this business.

Today, journalists and publicists alike must sing a lovelier song for their supper. Don't insult journalists' sense of professional dignity by assuming they're too lazy to cobble together their own segments. This is not to say that your bounty of excellent B-roll will go unappreciated. Quite the contrary, the more heavy lifting you can contribute to the story in the form of research, background, and actual edit-ready material like formatted visuals and exclusive quotes, the more effective you'll be. Just don't expect a lot of say in what runs and what doesn't.

In a modern market that's increasingly niched, it's also the journalist's job to know the audience. To understand what's on the horizon that will interest *their* demographic and produce stories that speak to those people in an engaging manner. After all, there are over 100 million cable subscribers in the US alone.

Moreover, the consumer audience is far savvier than ever before. This is not the 50's, when cigarettes could be sold as good for you: *If you really like to smoke a lot, why not make the change to Kent, today? Why not start with a carton?* Today, any hint of prefab bullshit has them reaching for the remote or turning the page.

You may get some off-peak filler slots for entire stories in the can, but helping journalists tailor their own will get you much farther.

DON'T
TAKE JOURNALISTS
FOR GRANTED.

You don't write! You don't call. You never even told me what you thought of the piece!

Sound like your mother? There's a difference: your mother will love you anyway. A busy, over-extended and, most importantly, *esteemed* editor or journalist—sifting through more pitches than he or she even has space to run—will not.

More so than most, the publicity industry relies on social grace and charm—in every sense of the word, *attractiveness*. Reporters, particularly at longer-lead publications, are accustomed to being courted. The magazine world (while perhaps not explicitly…) offers the opportunity for long-standing and *mutually* beneficial relationships.

One example:
There is a certain beauty industry queen, ____, an editorial pillar from *Glamour* who has been in the field for nearly forty years. Not surprisingly, she is also recognized as one of the most difficult women to appeal to, with time for very few. In my early years I encountered endless stonewalling tactics in my attempts to meet with her. Letter after letter, call after call, I was redi-

rected, humored, and finally pitied by her multi-tiered coven of assistants.

Frustrating.

Eventually, learning that her intriguing accent was Polish, I had a friend of mine translate a formal letter of greeting into Polish and sent it, priority messenger, to her attention. I knew the foreign characters would baffle her gatekeepers and she would be forced to read it herself. She was delighted by the resourcefulness and chutzpa, and to this day I am one of her favorite publicists, able to get an audience with her even on her most harried days.

So don't be stymied by initial resistance. At a certain level, it's to be expected. Do pursue a more clever approach, one that differentiates you from the rest. There is always a way in, though most often it has less to do with flattery or favors than discerning a soft spot, if you will—some particular individuality that is overlooked and can be massaged.

Then squeeze.

CHAPTER THREE

PITCHING

Most publicists don't know how to speak. Or pitch.

The fact is that most of the shills who call don't even know what they're talking about, let alone how to talk to a media contact. It's bad enough to waste people's time; many "publicists" seem determined to bore everyone as well.

Look at it this way: you've done it. You've made your way inside—wooed a client who needs your services and formulated an angle you're sure will appeal to the media. It's time to get your work in front of the public. Only one person stands between your message and the huddled masses yearning to wear your clients' perfume, sport their chronometers, or stay in their hotels. It is that person whom you are now about to call.

Your contact may wear the title of editor, producer, journalist or any number of other nomenclatures. Whatever they may be called, these people all have certain essentials in common, at least as far as you'll be concerned.

Foremost is that they get hundreds of calls a day very, very much like yours. How many of those calls do you suppose they remember for more than 45 seconds? ...favorably?

Pitching is about quality rather than quantity. You're the last thing on the mind of any of the contacts you reach. You must demonstrate within the first ten seconds of conversation that, unlike the idiot who just called about the plus size fashion show during fashion week (wink), you might, in fact, be of some concrete use.

So let us introduce the sound bite.

And short is the key word. It's a bite, not a buffet—a snappy little caplet of useful or provocative information. Its function: to arrest the surgical machinery of the average media maker's psyche long enough to pique a question or two.

After all, this is how the people you're talking to will be thinking. They want—need—to envision what the headline will read, how the newscaster (*their* newscaster) will segue into your segment, or how your blurb will fit with the news cycle. They don't need to know that you are "calling-from-the-award-winning-firm-of-so-and-so".

Here, then, are some things you DON'T do once you are ready to call. And what you would be better advised to do instead.

DON'T
PICK UP THE PHONE
YET.

Nothing is worse than actually getting through the phalanx of gatekeepers and voicemail screens surrounding the average decision maker, only to realize you had nothing real to say. You've finally got your "ring", and you proceed to blunder your way through a jumble of half-baked palaver so pathetically incoherent it arouses more annoyance than interest in your story.

Were you hoping to go straight to voicemail again? They have call display. Squander that initial entrée and you'll need to be representing Brangelina to hear the word 'hello' again.

Review your points. *Then* call.

Your first words should be well thought out and packed with content. If you get, for example, producers thinking, they'll start to shoot questions that allow them to shape your pitch to their show, their executive producer's demands, and any current projects they may have in the wings. Only thorough preparation on your part will sustain this dynamic. If you're unprepared to address every potential angle of an idea, you will simply miss avenues on which to sell it. If you stumble over the first few "what ifs" and "how abouts", your pitch may be viewed as one-dimensional, weak, or too much work for a story worth airing. Editors are much the same.

You need to be ready. Immerse yourself in what you plan to discuss before you call.

Nor should you expect to call someone up, get a green light, fork over a boilerplate release and head for cocktails. You are educating your contact on the topic regarding which you called. It's vital to be a valid, responsible, *responsive* source of information and insight. Your agility in discussing every aspect of a service or product reinforces the story's pertinence and makes you an authoritative source—on this as well as future projects.

And on that note:

DON'T
USE CANNED PHRASES.

The natural—and occasionally spoken—response to stale lead-ins like "How are you today" will be "Who the hell is this?" Don't say "the reason I'm calling today," or "I'm following up with you on..." or that you "just wanted to touch base."

Honestly. Such phrases are the appendix of conversation; if they did once serve some function, evolution has forgotten what. For you, they are more likely to produce the unseen rolling of eyes than anything of worth.

Using sales-y or cheesy expressions quickly forfeits what interest you've aroused in contacts who may well have been engaged in something *relevant* when you interposed with your call. Catch phrases come off as hackneyed rote. Like all decision makers, media executives are attuned to anything that smacks of a script. They'll ask you to leave voicemail, tell you they're not taking pitches right now, say they prefer email... Or simply hang up and get back to their deli salad and page proofs.

Wow. You've just spent the last 15 seconds orating into a dead phone.

Next time, proceed to the matter at hand without flourishes. If what you actually have to say is interesting, they'll certainly give you a moment of their time.

However, at magazines and some other media, lead times of weeks or months allow people more leisure for impromptu chat. What's being brainstormed in March may not reach newsstands until June. Terseness, where unneeded, comes across as brusque, and brusqueness will turn these contacts off more often than not. Be friendlier. Unless they sound distracted or stressed, take time to engage a little more deeply with them than you would with someone under the gun.

In television, especially in news and other live production, the lead time is drastically curtailed. The contact you've reached is probably on deadline for something due yesterday.

Get to the point.

DON'T DRONE THROUGH A SCRIPT.

You're calling to discuss ideas, not recite a speech. If you've mastered the ideas and considered their ramifications; if you've bothered to find out a little about the organization you're calling; if the referral comes from sources well-informed about your contact; then you can approach this conversation as you would with any other new acquaintance. The fact that you are initiating the discussion should never make so much difference that you recite your part like headlong Shakespeare.

Yes, you will at times be calling people cold, meaning that you have their numbers not through proper introduction, but some other channel. And yes, this may irritate some, especially if they attained their own positions without having to break much of a sweat. But no matter who sold you the script; no matter how well you once did peddling cutlery that could puncture a car door; canned lines still make you sound like a hapless kid dealing gimmicky knives.

At best, you might get asked to put your boss on the line for the real story.

You need to be absorbed enough in the concept that you can encapsulate it interestingly in 30 seconds or less and can then field questions. This should make it—and any other topic that comes up—easy to discuss *spontaneously,* like a living, breathing human being.

DON'T
BE UPTIGHT.

Being unnecessarily concise is only one way to send a signal that you are uncomfortable with the person you're addressing. Others are needless formality, affected pomposity and forms of address from the index pages of Emily Post.

Such behavior may be meant to convey stature and authority, or even deference, but it's seen for what it is: the apprehension of callow interlopers.

You come across as cold, aloof, supercilious, or tense, just when you need to establish rapport.

Of course, exaggerated congeniality and nonchalance are even worse. Nobody wants to be your pal. Not on the first date. Certainly you want to avoid coming across as too tightly laced, but nor should you seem too desperate to pass as footloose and freewheeling.

Be real, but act with respect. Understand that you're speaking with someone whose time is valuable and limited. This person may be working on a number of things in quick succession, some of them simultaneously, and possibly behind schedule.

This is not to say that you need be reflexively apologetic. Appearing obsequious or self-consciously deferential infers that you *are* wasting their time, and can position you as a groveling, inconsequential nuisance to those who are only too inclined to view you that way. Simply relay your dynamite idea with an enthusiasm and confidence that you *actually feel* in a charming, easy manner that's free of discomfort with your self-perceived status.

Forget about yourself and focus on your idea.

Respect people's time by making your idea worthwhile *to them*. When you know it is, think about why. When you know why, think about how to explain it to someone else. What are the benefits of this whole thing? What are they going to do for the contact's outlet? How cool is that?

Now pick up the phone.

DON'T
BE SHY.

On the phone, your voice replaces dress and written expression as the dead litmus of your personality, and subconsciously speaks volumes. Being clear and positive will satisfy the first test: are you confident? Confidence denotes success, and *success* sells soap. And diamonds. And travel packages to Florence...

You mumble. You stammer. You trail off in mid-sentence, or... *I don't know... I mean, like, you know? Or whatever.* Maybe you're all too aware, but this is the impression shyness and nervousness make over the phone. That you are unprepared, confused, flaky or noncommittal.

It's one thing to see you blush and bat your lashes as you search for the word "the". It's another to wait while you figure out what you're doing on the telephone, since you can't simply cut your losses and proffer a box of chocolates. We all have things to do with our day, and if you're painfully shy, on the phone you'll just be painful, period.

So, relax. Anyone still on the line may want to hear what you have to say.

Confidence also surpasses beauty as a draw. You will find this true in those you date (hopefully), admire or witness meeting great success. How many times has the sound of someone's voice made you wonder how they looked?

Being "good" on the phone means projecting a positive image for your listener. When you emanate confidence, people respond. A focused, sharp, dynamic attitude encourages your listener to regard you, thus your ideas, with respect.

Whether you achieve this pluck through industry acumen, charisma, boldness or a combination of those winning traits, confidence is the linchpin of any pitch. Before you get on the phone to start the first discussion, stop to remind yourself why your story is a great one.

We'll all be glad you did.

DON'T
EVER PUT ME ON
SPEAKERPHONE
WITHOUT ASKING.

Understand? If you do I may just call your boss, not you. Gaining a client or colleague's confidence and approval never involves making them feel self-conscious, and no one is favorably impressed by the idea that you're too busy to hold a receiver or too lazy to relay a conversation to others involved.

If you behave without grace or lack basic etiquette your clients will simply find more appealing people to work with.

Using the speakerphone implies that the person on the other end does not merit your attention or effort. Moreover, basic telephone decorum includes manifest discretion. One always affords a business contact the basic courtesy of picking up the phone. Not that you should expect to amaze anyone by answering with the receiver, only that people will be affected in the negative should you not.

Outside of conference calls with everyone announced, when unavoidably using both hands elsewhere (for what, I can't imagine), or in some emergency, the speakerphone is gauche. If you must use it, do inform your listener and by all means apologize.

Some really do need these finer points of tact explained. Don't be one them.

DON'T ROCK YOUR DRAWL.

If New York City prides itself on one strength other than being the standard for all that is culturally paramount, it is on being an emporium of all that is, period. "Why go anywhere else," New Yorkers ask, "when we have the whole world right here?" Don't suppress your accent! Just round it off a bit. Editors like variety, too, insofar as it falls under their approval. It is, after all, their stock in trade.

That said, you'll want to 'less'n yer Tex-ass. New Yorkers have trouble taking strong regional accents terribly seriously—even their own. No, *particularly* their own. On a call, there is no visual context for your NASCAR twang or your big, Bronx honk and, the truth is, people's assumptions tend toward the unfavorable. Let me count the ways: that you are uneducated or (worse) unsophisticated; that you may be belligerent or pushy; that you are crass or lack the sensibilities of the milieu to which you seek entrée.

As surely as hand-tooled Tony Lamas or beauty pageant grooming, strong accents, brusque mannerisms, or extremes of pace and pitch define you in such a way as to undermine credibility, and thus business, during Monday morning meetings at the Carlyle.

Your full, Fran Drescher brogue is best saved for shore leave. Turn it down from 11 to the low fives; more and better doors will open. If you're Southern, think Old Sewanee, which even the sniffiest Manhattanite cannot resist. If you're from the Midwest, just try not to blurt out too many Uff-das.

No matter where you're from, if your natural vernacular and intonation come off as less than urbane, refine your speech toward the elegant. You need to *sound* like you know what you're talking about. Then you'll actually be listened to, not just heard.

Foster a tone that blends resonance with reserve, and you'll do just fine.

DON'T
FORGET TO WRITE.

A call that achieves tangible results (read: press) for you represents a favor from your media contact. Your contacts realize this fact no matter how graciously they may feign to overlook it. A call followed up only by the next pitch resembles a Saturday night date followed up only with another Thursday afternoon query. The timing is somehow suspect.

Wham, bam, thank you, Ma'am is never a shrewd approach to a (long term) relationship.

Saying thank you with another call might be awkward. E-mail says, "Your assistance is *this* important to me: CLICK-CLICK." It places you comfortably among the legion of hacks styling themselves publicists. Place yourself among gracious professionals, instead.

Have you ever received a proper thank you note? Written on quality stationary with a postmark and everything? It made you feel special, did it not? People genuinely enjoy being noted for their efforts.

In business, there are myriad reasons to send a thank you note: for a good professional turn, in response to a referral, after a job interview, or when you have been treated to lunch by a contact or similarly entertained by your boss. Less and less common in our manic age of email, texting, BlackBerries and mobile phones, it's a classically courteous and a nearly effortless way to define yourself as considerate and well mannered.

Above all, never type a thank you note: it is not "more business-like", it's just "less charming". The recipient will assume you lack either legible penmanship or simple grace. Use company letterhead and a matching envelope, and they'll suppose you lack either taste or proper stationery.

Invest in quality 5 x 7 correspondence cards or fold-over notes in a style that balances classicism with modern simplicity. Tasteful personal touches—your name, initials, an elegant border—are never out of place. Sidestep anything florid, homespun, metallic, overly personalized, or with the words 'thank you' printed on it.

Your message should be simple, succinct and forward-looking. Punctuation is important. Don't begin with 'thank you', but rather, what you most appreciate about the person having taken the time to work with you and how you look forward to future endeavors. Then thank them and close, on a new line, with "Best", "Best regards" or "Sincerely". Sign your name in a confident hand and, if necessary, toss in your business card. Always use the honorific when addressing an envelope—*Mr. John Smith,* not *John Smith*—and post within 5 days of the event.

A gracious gesture of appreciation, your thoughtfulness will set you apart, accrue good will and aid in your success. In writing thank-you notes to others for their efforts, you are recognized for your own. It's win-win.

And since we seem to be on the subject of writing...

DON'T
UZ F***ING :P
(; SMILEYS!!! ;D

This also applies to more than one exclamation point at a time (better yet, more than one per message). It also applies to candy-colored stationery, inks or e-mail characters. Do I hav 2 menshN IM tXt?

IMHO, U R a 2L 4 EvR UZN it.

If your goal is to portray yourself as a randomly directed, attention-deficit post-adolescent, any of these methods are superb. Multiple exclamation points and impressionistic punctuation are especially effective in giving your correspondence the look and feel of a sorority bulletin board. It's the emoticon school of writing, and it's not advantageous to you nor appropriate to an adult environment.

If you wish to interest anyone in well, *anything,* you'll need to grow up. Utilize your spell check program or (idea!) just learn to spell. Start communicating in human language rather than international hospitality symbols.

Important and timely information demands the precision, nuance and grace afforded by proper language.

In New York City, this generally means media standard English. English is the example for this book, but what I'm saying applies to them all. Media standard, in case you IM'd through English 101, means that you write primarily in *sentences* with a complete *subject* and *verb* (yes, they're on Wikipedia). It means capital letters are used for well-defined, grammatical purposes, while punctuation and spelling also follow common rules.

When even your routine e-mail correspondence exploits the power of conventional spelling, syntax and contextual logic, you send a message within each message: what you have to say is important enough to merit consideration. You also acknowledge your readers as sophisticated, intelligent and serious, able to appreciate well-conceived concepts and dialogue. Write like you mean to be taken seriously, and you will be.

Even on the Internet.

DON'T WRITE LIKE YOU KNOW ME.

Remember, you don't yet. Chances are anyone you're pitching via e-mail is busy, reviews several hundred messages daily, and has a healthy distaste for grammatical mistakes and inane banter. They are of the species already discussed, with an added contempt for sloppy written expression, cloying familiarity and, by extension, smileys. When presenting yourself via e-mail, understand the mental state of those whose interest you are attempting to attract.

Or at least don't presume that you do.

The more assumptions you make, the more widely you may miss the mark. Don't assume, even in the more pop-intensive reaches of the media-scape, that you can address a lot of casual phrasing and breezy slang to someone whom you haven't met. You don't know anyone until you've interacted with them. Repeatedly. As a rule, it may take as many five interactions for a contact even to remember you.

See that your letter is written in a respectful, accurate and clear tone. The person reviewing your email probably may havet significantly more experience than you. Brevity, respect and enthusiasm are key. Relevance is paramount. So is proper use of capital letters.

This is not to say you need to be excessively formal. The loquaciousness of a liberal arts grad from Indiana (sorry, Indiana) trying to pass in literary society looks no better in writing than it sounds on the phone. Let your style flow smoothly, your sentences unfold directly, and your observance of the rules serve elegance of expression rather than the other way around. Approach people without trepidation—just respect.

A message composed in a grammatical, well sequenced, articulate style and everyday language should achieve all of this. Cordiality and anticipation are perfectly appropriate in opening and concluding. Neutrality in the rest of the message keeps people focused on your

pitch, rather than wondering where they're sup-
posed to know you from.

DON'T CLICK "SEND" YET.

Grammatical errors reflect negatively and significantly endanger your first impression. Either
you lack education, are unfamiliar with common terminologies and products in the industry
you're attempting to promote, or are too slapdash to get it right.

Before you even address the message, back slowly
away from the keyboard! Are you long-winded
and indistinct? Are the dates and times correct?
If you've cut and pasted from another message,
have you changed names and locations? Have
you at least observed the rules in this book?

If you haven't yet read over the message, chances
are that not all of these details will be check out.
If you have, confirm that you've said everything
as succinctly as you could. Is there a turn of
phrase that's too clever or that falls flat? Is the
information arresting enough to merit more than
perfunctory attention?

And for God's sake, use spell check.

Here you make the difference between presenting the same image in writing that a sharp suit, polished shoes and good posture would create in person—and the impression that missing buttons, stained shirt and a tatty friendship bracelet would leave. Editing your communications—even getting feedback—is one more way to give yourself an edge. Respect for your own work demonstrates respect for the intelligence, attention and time of your colleagues, clients and contacts.

It's a simple tenet of professionalism.

CHAPTER FOUR

FACE TIME

You've heard the platitudes: 80% of business today is transacted by telephone. In the Internet Age, commerce takes place any time of day or night between people who may never even meet. Smart phones and wireless allow us instant access to our contacts and data, no matter where we are. Well and good, as far as it goes.

It just doesn't go nearly as far as the latest gadget guru would have you believe. Even an increasingly global village is still a village, perhaps nowhere more than New York City. Even if you sleep with a Bluetooth clipped to your ear, are glued to an office laptop and obsessive about your Blackberry, publicity's bread and butter is still made face to face with clients and the contacts you want to put *them* in front of. It is *public* relations.

Define who's who, and what's what. Identify the various media and their component business verticals. Consider the common business structures within those media as well as what business style prevails in each and who holds sway at every level. The distinctions between various subcategories of broadcast, print and digital media, worlds unto themselves in many ways, are important.

FOUR PS

Whichever medium you target, success is more likely if you remember what I refer to as the Four Ps: Presentation, Preparation, Professionalism and Promises. The first three qualities relate to several further areas we're addressing in other chapters. You may tire of these reminders, but never weary in applying them to every aspect of what you do. You'll never regret the effort.

As to the latter, an ability to follow through on commitments made, particularly in face-to-face meetings, has a direct bearing on the level of respect clients and contacts have for you. Your value to these people is as only great as the worth of your promises.

Finally, as the publicist it is your role, when presenting a client to a contact, to function as a moderator between the two, not as a direct participant yourself. It requires tact and alertness to know when to interject and, more importantly, when not to.

Once you've interested a contact enough in your client to get the two in the same room for a talk, you've arrived at the last and most crucial moment before closing the deal. Take some time to consider the following pointers, and try not to cock it up.

DON'T
FORGET YOUR
MANNERS.

Nothing will distinguish you more regrettably than forgetting them. This is New York City. Contrary to popular belief, people hold doors for each other here almost on reflex. Try sneezing on the subway without hearing at least one "Bless you." *Excuse me. Thank you. Have a nice day.* You'll hear these phrases every bit as frequently here as anywhere else in America, even if occasionally uttered with a Big Apple edge.

So when you've taken up forty-five minutes of some established media maker's day, disappeared from sight without so much as a word of acknowledgment and reappear only the next time there's something she can do for you, don't expect top priority.

Start with a thank you message the minute you're back at your desk.

Promptly thanking someone for a favor is the single easiest thing you can do to stay on that person's radar. Research has shown that it takes at least five interactions with someone new before we begin to feel a sense of familiarity. Just to move up in the count, a quick thank you note is a no-brainer.

It also gives you an opportunity to recap any agreed-upon next steps. Again, the decision makers you deal with may be scheduling their days down to the minute. For most people it is tremendously difficult under such conditions to track every action item in their week, let alone their month. A brief note to thank and recap deftly reinforces any commitments they have made while enhancing the familiarity quotient.

Mention that you enjoyed the meeting and express your appreciation for the time and attention. Cite the topic for context, reiterate your next steps, state your availability for any issues or questions that may come up prior to your next meeting, and express your anticipation in the meantime.

E-mail is fine. Short, sweet and bullshit-free is *de rigueur*.

DON'T WASTE TIME APPEALING TO THE IRRELEVANT.

Remember: you aren't just investing your own time preparing for this meeting. You're also asking clients to turn precious hours away from their core business in order to orient you on their message, collaborate on a winning presentation and prepare for a face-to-face meeting with someone they hope will pass decisive judgment on what they are offering. If you then proceed to drag them across town to a meeting that turns out to be with someone's assistant, they're unlikely to be impressed with you. The same is true of appointments with someone in the wrong department.

As a publicist, connections are your stock in trade. Your value plummets if you don't offer direct access to those who can put your clients, or their product, in the public eye. You will have to warm up a few gatekeepers to reach anyone with clout, but that's your job. Wait until you've performed it *before* you get any clients involved. A misconceived meeting serves only to undermine *your* standing and waste *their* time.

So who are these high value contacts? In different media they have different titles; these will vary somewhat even between organizations within a single medium. However, the chart on **page 75** offers a general idea of common broadcast organizational structures, job titles and responsibilities in the verticals you'll need to scale. Use it to secure conversations, desk-sides and interviews with the correct contact at the right stage of the game.

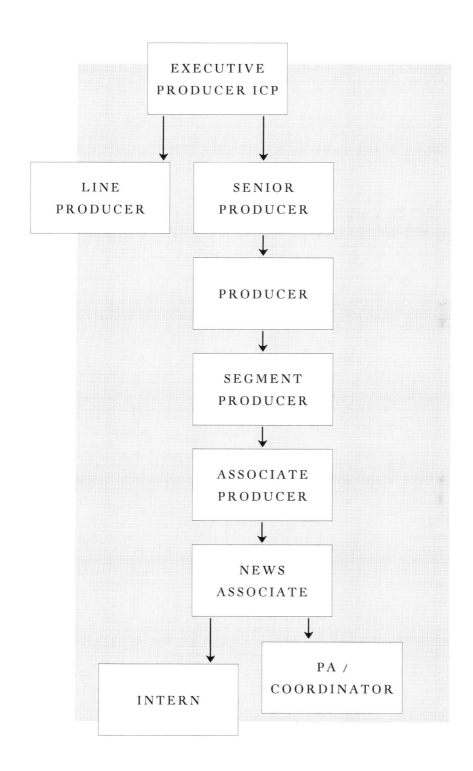

DON'T
WASTE A GREAT PITCH
MAKING IT JUST ONCE.

It's a tough world. You just spent weeks putting together a pitch, angling for a meeting with the style editor at a prestigious publication, and finally got ten minutes in her office. Only to have her tell you it just wasn't right for their upcoming issues. So it's time to salve your wounds with a double Hendrick's and crawl back to the drawing board, right?

Not yet.

Have you contacted the sections editor? What about the online editor? Have you considered working your client into a feature on a broader topic? If not, you might want to hold off on the consolation shots and get back on the phone instead. Next time, broaden your efforts from the start, rather than limiting them to one person per institution.

The same story or pitch can often be targeted to a number of different contacts within the same outlet. A bright, young musician whose album release doesn't seem pressing enough for an entertainment feature might work perfectly embedded in a fashion piece on entertainers' personal style. The nutritionist you're grooming for daytime talk shows may score just as much interest in her new holistic cooking site from the producer of an evening news hour as from the lifestyle program where you'd most like her to appear.

Make a list from the outset that prioritizes relevant contacts in descending order. Put feelers out to all of them in succession and develop those who respond most favorably. If your top choice declines, turn to the next person rather than give up on a great idea because an editor at Condé Nast didn't call you back.

Hedge your bets. You'll spend more time placing stories and less placing drink orders in the middle of the day.

DON'T
BE LATE.

You thought it would take you just 20 minutes. You hadn't expected the subways to be this infrequent at 11:00 AM. You thought your client could keep up on the stairs. You thought your contact called ahead to security! And dear God, you had no idea of the difference between 45 and 65% humidity.

By this point, there's no way to enter with grace. Remember that next time you stretch a call out ten minutes longer instead of grabbing your bag and hailing a taxi.

And I do mean taxi. The subway is fantastic for getting around on your own or with those you know well, but not the best call with a client. New York may boast America's foremost transit system, but that's not saying much. Manhattan subways are almost perennially under construction, generally crowded and, often as not, rife with junk food and unappetizing smells. Yes, it's a wonder they exist at all after 150 years of deferred maintenance. No, they will not reliably get you to an important meeting in the condition you need to be in.

In summer, New York humidity turns every platform into a literal sauna. In winter, they're swamps of gray muck and slush. If you've taken my shoe advice in Chapter 1, you won't subject even your shoes to this.

Worse, taking the subway makes you look cheap —or broke.

Show clients what they're paying for. Spring for a cab. Calculate your trip from door to door, including elevators and security checks, which alone can take a quarter of an hour. Calculate how long it will take you. Then add fifteen minutes.

What does this priceless example teach us? How about not going in blind without an agenda or talking points, or dressed like a slob?

Know your target and prepare accordingly. To help you and your client stay on the same page, create a "one-sheet" profile on the media contact with whom you are meeting. Learn the contact's history and background in advance. Find out what they've written or produced recently, define areas of focus, anything helpful that Google might yield, &c.

Next, shape a set of talking points around this profile—elements essential to client's core message with key angles to emphasize during the meeting as well as to revisit with your contact afterward. A detailed agenda allows you to hold sway over the conversation, avoid pointless repetition, preclude awkward pauses, maintain an easy flow of ideas and, most importantly, productively utilize everyone's time.

Better preparation makes for better interviews. It demonstrates respect for the contact you are looking to work with as well as for client you are representing, while framing you in a positive light as a professional communicator.

DON'T
HOG THE LIMELIGHT,
DEAR.

So, you hit it off fabulously with a new contact. The two of you have so much in common it's uncanny. He laughs his head off at all of your jokes and shares the latest dish from TV land. You're really hoping to impress everyone in the room today with your breezy social skills and quick wit. But guess what?

He's got to get to his next appointment now, and your client has barely said three words.

Business should be fun, and it is your job to put everyone at ease so the dialogue runs smoothly. But there's a difference between a business and a social call, and only idiots and amateurs confuse the two. The point of this occasion is to flaunt your client's superlative qualities, not your own. As the publicist, you're here to moderate a discussion, not appear as its centerpiece.

You need to be on the sidelines, PERIOD. Clients pay you to display *them* to their best advantage. This cannot be accomplished if you are grandstanding or thoughtlessly dominating the conversation.

Deliver them well prepped, but remember: your clients are the experts here. Any contributions you make should only support and promote their authority on the matter, not outshine it. If you can set up an opportunity for your client during the meeting, by all means do so. If there's a question you think could be asked or an aside that casts favorable light, interject. Briefly.

The rest of the time, just sit there, look good, observe, take notes, and keep quiet.

DON'T
GET OFF TOPIC.

It's also easy to sit there nodding every few moments and letting the conversation slide pleasantly by while surreptitiously regarding the attractive assistant from the corner of your eye. Do this long enough, and you may find your contact genially wrapping things up, telling your client they're working on a number of things and will be in touch.

What just happened?

They seemed to be having such a good time! What did your client say? Or not say? Where did the conversation go? Unfortunately, you have no idea, and it's too late to catch up.

It's one thing take the back seat in a meeting. It's another to zone out. The difference between the two is a little thing called poise.

In meetings, the key to professionalism is to listen carefully. Keep close track of what clients are saying, what they should be saying and, most importantly, what the media contact may be indicating, even indirectly. You show your mettle by sussing out how your client can be of most use to the reporter, editor or producer that you are meeting with.

This is the reason both you and the client prepared so carefully, doing your homework to develop a one-sheet and talking points, going over everything backward and forward. Of course, a sharp and socially fluid client who finds a way to hit every angle is a joy to work with.

However, even the sharpest miss a beat now and then. Gently redirect as needed, stepping in to prompt whenever you see them about to miss a great chance to make themselves relevant, mediating when people start to talk past each other.

And make sure to get that assistant's desk-line before you leave.

DON'T
LET CLIENTS GET
OFF TRACK.

Just as you can showboat, over-schmooze and otherwise lose focus, so can your client. One who is hitting it off too splendidly with the contact may be missing chances to reinforce the message. Another, content to bray about personal achievements or the superiority of a particular item (i.e., the one the client sells), has strayed from pleasant, incidental banter into the margins of off-putting braggadocio or irrelevance. And clients who are nervous or prickly are on difficult footing from the word go.

These are the situations where you can show your stuff, prompting the client with questions and suggestions as needed, navigating rough patches, and boosting confidence. Get behind them like a coach; help them demonstrate their value to the contact while steering clear of gratuitous self-aggrandizement.

DON'T
BE A FLAKE, SIR.

Not following through is unprofessional. If you don't actually *have* any promises to keep by the end of a meeting, if things wind down with no sense of purpose or what happens next, you've failed to do your job. Don't expect indulgence from a nationally respected editor who barely knows you. This is not a social call.

Most of all, don't expect business if you aren't prepared to do the work.

When a meeting with a contact ends, hopefully your job is just beginning. Briefly recap what was covered, outline any next steps and identify yourself as the resource for quotes, pictures or further interviews. Then explicitly establish who's going to be doing what next, and when the next point of contact will be.

Taking longer than 24 hours to follow through on all identified terms is unacceptable. People will generally have schedules that render anything outside a one-day window—against the backdrop of everything else they have to get done—difficult to remember. Immediacy is paramount. There's no single factor that will distinguish you more sharply than your unfailing ability to deliver what you say when you say you will.

DON'T OVERSTAY YOUR WELCOME.

If you're sitting there after the meaningful business is done, filling the air with your own voice or allowing your client to do so, you've begun to work the finish off what could otherwise have been a polished piece. If you're still fielding questions and wandering in ever-widening circles of small talk after getting buy-in on your key commitments, you're providing people with material for second thoughts.

Rapport is important. *Start* by establishing it. Once a deal is sealed, you only raise the risk of reversal by lingering too long in the afterglow. At best, you obscure the core business in a fog of superfluous chitchat. At worst, you annoy people who have other matters they should already have been attending to. Recognize when the meeting has reached its conclusion and bring it to a close.

It is not a bad idea to ask at the outset how much time your contact has to devote to the meeting.

That way you'll have a convenient moment to look at your watch and note that it's time you were getting on to your next appointment—whether you have one or not.

It's never a problem if you have other commitments waiting. Its simple prudence to cut a meeting short that's dragging after relevant points have been addressed. Editors and reporters understand, clients feel important and valued as well, and best of all, you look like your time is sought after.

Once you've established what the next steps are and made sure everyone knows whom to contact in regard to what, initiate a few concluding pleasantries and get out the door on a high note.

CHAPTER FIVE

COCKTAILS
AND
SOCIALIZING

According to the *Encyclopedia of New York City,* the island's original, Native American inhabitants affectionately referred to it as *manahacht-anienk,* meaning "general state of inebriation". Whether they meant themselves or their new, Dutch neighbors over on what we now call Broadway is... hazy in retrospect.

No surprise then that Wall Street was named for a rampart that the more virtuous 17th-Century citizens of New Amsterdam erected partly to stem the tide of soused English colonists and other stray flotsam attracted by the abundance of pubs in the area. True to its beginnings, New York City to this day boasts more watering holes per block than any other city in the world.

In true form, business, and any other activity, in New York, often involves imbibing. A world-class city filled with world-class drinkers, it's an intoxicating metropolis in many ways. At the forefront of everything, commerce to cocktails, in the de facto cultural center of America even the signature cocktail is loaded—with history.

The Manhattan was named after the Manhattan Club, a bastion of upper crust Democrats, and first mixed for Samuel J. Tilden, elected Governor of New York in 1874. A presidential hopeful, Tilden was later embroiled in the 19th Century's greatest election scandal when he won the popular vote against Republican Rutheford B. Hayes but was denied the White House based on crafty ballot counting in Florida (sound familiar?)

Fifty years later, when Prohibition reformers straitjacketed America for over a decade, New York responded by debuting 100,000 speakeasies. As the city's patron saint, Frank Sinatra, once put it, "I feel sorry for people who don't drink. When they wake up in the morning, that's as good as they're going to feel all day."

Which is more or less how New Yorkers feel.

Publicity, for its part, is a profession intricately entwined with fashion, media, entertainment and, excepting the financial industry, outdone only by those three fields, in a race to the nearest bar for business meetings and professional events.

For *your* part, the list of picturesque drinkers is long—the messy drunk, the maudlin drunk, the bitter drunk—and you don't want on it. If you've had any problems in the past managing alcohol's effects, deal with that before starting in business here.

In New York, perhaps more than other cities, it can be difficult to distinguish between a night on the town cutting loose with friends and one forging bonds with professional associates. For those in marketing and *public* relations, the distinction is worth noting. Moreover, in a city where functioning alcoholics and social critics routinely overlap, how and *what* you drink will classify you. Use this to your advantage. Or at least avoid neglecting it to your detriment.

If you please, a few specifics:

DON'T
ORDER VILE HOOCH.

The following drinks are trashy, some more than others, all more than enough. Here are the top 5 mistakes, and the caption broadcast with your order:

> WHITE ZIN: Drink up! I have to catch a train back to the Island in time for *American Idol.*

> AMARETTO SOURS: To all my sister-rrrrrrrrs! ohmigodIwill *never.* Forget you guys. Whenwegraduate.

> JACK – OR ANYTHING ELSE – AND COKE: See above, minus four years.

7 AND 7: Third rate scotch *alone* doesn't cut it for *me*. Only fizzy sugar water brings it up to *my* level.

RAIL DRINKS WITH JUICE (YES, EVEN GIN AND JUICE AND VODKA CRAN-BERRY): Bling-bling, muthaf*cka! Yo, light anotha-N-let's holla at the DJ. (*Subtitle: "I may be a pasty dude with a Yankees cap and clipper burns on the neck, but I'm still down."*)

These drinks betray a tawdry history. They are sweet; they are cloying. They are meant for palates raised on Pringles and Pepsi. They also indicate that, having staggered all the way from the trunk of Dad's car on prom night to your best friend's frat porch after commencement, your sense of taste has crumpled in a heap.

Succinctly: forget the junk mixology. Order like a grown up.

The famous maxim, "God is in the details", actually derives from a German saying which sites the Devil instead. Either way, it's certainly true of drinks. Seeming trifles, yet loaded with subtext, some cocktails are best avoided.

To begin with, anything sugary, mixed with Coke, Seven-Up, milk, curaçao or grenadine, equipped with an umbrella, served in a parfait glass or, except the Manhattan and the Negroni, garnished with a cherry. These rules also apply to martinis, which are ordered in their classic form or not at all.

With their inelegant connotations, cloying details are more prom night than posh, and served rather to greenhorns than the graceful. Again, let's outgrow the swanky mixotica.

Champagne is appropriate for holidays, celebrations and, women, as an evening cocktail. New York imports excellent wines from every corner of the world and good advice can be gleaned from the shopkeepers devoted to sourcing them. Brush up with a classic like *The Wine Bible*. In any case, choose well when handed the restaurant wine list or en route to a dinner party.

Quality spirits are generally served neat, though there is some wiggle room in that. While no one knowledgeable would put ice in a 25 year old scotch, you won't offend good taste by ordering a premium vodka on the rocks.

Tip well. Always remove the stir stick or straw. Wine glasses are held by the stem, not the bowl; and all drinks in the left hand, so your right is warm, dry and free to shake hands.

DON'T DRESS DOWN FOR DRINKS.

Especially if you're in a junior position. At this stage of the game, you're a long way from choosing your own opportunities and must be ready to capitalize on every possibility regardless of how randomly it presents itself. Every evening at bars across the city, vital contacts are made and relationships cemented; none of them will be yours if you're telegraphing that you've already punched the clock.

Your appearance is the easiest way to control how you are perceived. Appearing as put-together and professional after work as you do during the day signals to those around you that you're still in the game during overtime. Maintaining a sense of propriety shows respect for your guests or hosts, as well as yourself and those you work for.

DON'T
GET AHEAD OF THE
OTHERS.

Gauge how others are pacing themselves and adjust your own stride accordingly. If your colleague, contact or client, is on their first drink while you're waving down a third, they'll assume that you're nervous, more focused on getting liquored than what they have to say, or worse, unaware that you have a drinking problem. Overindulgence in the professional realm smacks of dependence, boredom or anxiety—not qualities anyone admires in a business contact. Rather than downing a succession of martinis in an untoward stab at swift inebriation, have one or two and show the presence of mind to appreciate them.

With or without a business angle, cocktail hour is about enjoying a shared experience. The better you reflect the group's tempo and dynamic, the better you will be received. When such gatherings do have a professional dimension, the winning participant fosters congeniality without losing sight of the overall context or what defines proper use of an expense account. They don't keep summoning the server until they embarrass themselves, their cohorts or both.

DON'T
GET AHEAD OF YOUR-
SELF, EITHER.

Alcohol is a powerful social lubricant, and over indulgence makes for a slippery slope. There is a fine line between relaxed-and-charming and loose-and-louche. Drinking too much can easily render you unappealingly chummy, even indiscreet, to those less inebriated than you.

Though business imbibing is generally related to socializing (people gathering where alcohol is served), the expectations are *vastly* different. If you're clapping superiors on the back or boisterously holding forth, you're too swozzled for gracious conversation and not meeting those expectations.

Business is conducted at all hours in NYC, and certainly in the evening over cocktails. While it's crucial to be able to nurture relationships socially, it must be approached constructively. Stay crisply *en pointe*. Anticipate that those with you will have two or three cocktails and stay within those limits yourself. If someone else has five or six, this is no time for a test of Viking prowess. Distinguish yourself with good cheer— and innate decorum.

DON'T
TEXT.

It's so easy, so *tempting* to sneak a tiny break from conversation to peek at that incoming message about your dinner plans. Please resist. Turning your attention from someone in mid-conversation to fixate on a blinking plastic gadget exhibits you have either the focus of a house fly or are bored with the conversation and, even better, too impolite to disguise it. Your distraction signals that while they may be fully invested in the dialogue, *you* have better things to do.

Just as with a telephone call, if you must make plans or communicate some brief information, simply excuse yourself, step out and take care of it. Swiftly. Once the matter has been addressed, turn the device off—that's right, *off*—and return to the meeting. Continuous electronic interference, regardless of the cause, is rude. And will be taken as especially so if the person you're with came of age before MySpace.

In the highly interactive world of publicity, you want superiors and clients to feel that you are fully invested in every relationship. Offering your complete attention, with steady eye contact and incisive verbal engagement, is vital whether there's a drink in your hand or not.

DON'T
GAS ON ABOUT YOUR
TRIP TO CABO.

The novelists' advice to "write about what you know" applies just as well to conversation. But in both cases it's only a winning formula if you know things that are actually of interest to anyone other than yourself. An exchange focused exclusively on your own scintillating life is not an exchange at all and will bore people. One good definition of 'charm', a somewhat intangible quality, is that it's the ability to convey how interesting *the person you're speaking with* is and not how interesting *you* are.

Meanwhile, New York is an incredible resource, a cosmopolitan, international city in which countless people with an infinite variety of experiences will surround you. So ask questions. You'll learn more about the ins and outs of your trade—who's who, what's what, how things really get done here—from the opinions, stories and gossip of practiced industry veterans than you ever gleaned from a Communications textbook.

Don't squander these opportunities by babbling on pointlessly about yourself. This is not to say you shouldn't offer your own remarks; only that you should make clever use of the wisdom available to you *while* simultaneously charming peers with a flattering yet not obsequious interest in them and their expertise. You thus denote not only interest in their world but sincere, analytic curiosity—a quality prized in any profession.

Don't grill people relentlessly, though. Conversation is a gentle art. Without being tiresome or nosy, ask questions, follow up with queries, and venture conclusions of your own based on their responses. Interweave your experience with their own; find common ground and interests; if someone asks your opinion, respond briefly and pass a question back. Displaying a true interest in others is always appealing while, from a purely Machiavellian standpoint, the more you know about those in your field, the more adept you'll be at defining how they might assist with your career.

Of course, a dialogue with professional peers needn't be a one-way crash course on your shared profession, nor pertain exclusively to business interests; it just needs to be interesting. If you would like anyone of consequence to indulge in extended discussions with you, you must be able to hold up your end when it is time for you to speak.

A sophisticated individual is well rounded, capable of engaging on a range of topics. Consider your audience. In New York, as the writer Tom Wolfe once put it "Culture just seems to be in the air, like part of the weather" <http://en.wikipedia.org/wiki/Tom_Wolfe>. Being able to toss out an amusing aside on some starlet's latest imbroglio is one thing–arguably, that's what celebrities are there for–but pop culture as the *only* level on which you're genuinely conversant is another.

Cultivate finer sources of information than *Access Hollywood*, and a broader understanding of current events. Avoid confining your read of style magazines and throwaway novels. Include gallery exhibits and theatre performances in your list of diversions–or at least read key reviews so you have a working knowledge of who and what is culturally relevant and why.

Oh, yes: this works on dates, too.

DON'T MAKE BLATANT SEXUAL OVERTURES IN PUBLIC.

If you would like to portray yourself as someone with zero restraint, a blithe fool enslaved to baser desires, then you should blatantly hit on the bartender or server—or anyone else—in plain view of your work associates.

Now is not the time to discuss what traveling in packs will do for your sex life, and in some groups—especially male ones—nailing whatever looks most available is a sanctioned team sport. If your superiors engage in this pastime you won't be censured for participating. But generally your sex life should be handled in a circumspect manner when socializing with business colleagues and, most particularly, with anyone of higher rank.

Keep your dalliances at a distance. If the entire office is privy to the details of your shallowest sexual exploits, you will inevitably lose face. A casual tryst is not worth deglazing your mystique for. Maintain the advantage conferred by keeping a polished, professional distance between your business and personal exploits.

If you come across someone you find appealing while meeting business associates in a bar, take a circumspect approach. Chat them up briefly, share a quick drink at the bar, by all means exchange cards, but do not make it the focus of your evening. If you make plans to meet someone later, do so when business colleagues are out of earshot and do not bray about it afterward. Particularly if "later" is in two hours at your place. Such interaction should always be addressed discretely and outside the purview of your professional circle.

Should the object of your affection happen to work in the establishment, clearly no expediency is called for. Whatever carnal intentions the Ford-model-level bartender has made clear, whatever play you've decided to make for the comely creature that served your table all night, should be no one's business but your own.

Wait to focus on your follow up plans until your cohorts have departed. Escort them out, feign that you're heading home, and then discreetly double back for that off-the-clock swoop at your enticing new acquaintance. If you're feeling exceptionally mature, enjoy an after-hours flirtation, exchange numbers and arrange to have lunch later that week. If not, well, no one's the wiser.

DON'T
BE A PRETENTIOUS
TWIT.

Are there varying levels of character, sophistication and accomplishment among people? Certainly. But no one is beneath surmounting a rudimentary milieu, and no one is above regarding others with respect. It is unseemly to look down on anyone. A supercilious attitude says more about you than the subject of your contempt and has no place in the realm of good manners.

This may be applied to any and all with whom you come into contact in the daily course of doing business—interns, doormen, barmaids, the courier guy, waiters, office cleaning ladies, or your receptionist.

As a rule, you should not view bar staff as convenient, if 'common', sexual supplicants waiting to be picked off like skeet. Unless you wish to come off as a boor, you do not refer to female bartenders as "barwenches", other human beings as "the help", view taxi drivers are miscreants, or deem staff of any stripe inherently 'beneath' you.

Pandering to some presupposed caste system is distasteful and what it signifies about your perspective unattractive. These people may be otherwise toiling at any of the personally- if not financially-rewarding vocations (artist, writer, actor, take your pick) that draw creative people to Manhattan and make it such a fascinating city in which to live. Or they may be just decent citizens making a living.

Displaying disdain, even just amongst your colleagues, marks you as a pretentious ass to those who know better while aligning you with the sniggering yobs who do not.

DON'T BE THE LAST TO LEAVE.

Nothing is quite as pitiable as clinging to a stool and your last remaining co-worker's sleeve, pleading "just one more!" as a weeknight crowd dissipates along with the last of your associates. Remaining glued to the bar, imposing on a colleague to squeeze one more cocktail onto the expense tab in a half empty room advertises that you are either drunk, lack self-possession, have no better place to be, or all three. Maybe you really are that lonely. Why shout it from the rafters?

With or without cocktails, this business can be tricky and tough, but earning and maintaining the high regard of your colleagues and superiors is crucial to advancement.

Don't linger. Every situation has a beginning, a middle and an end. Note group cues: glancing at watches, passing up rounds, departing in twos and threes. Be among the first two thirds to leave. On a weekend this infers that you've got a life, places to go and people to see that others can only guess at. During the week, when you may have more to accomplish before turning in or want get the jump on tomorrow's goals, it indicates that you're conscious of time and use it productively.

Moreover, by walking out *with* people, bantering and exchanging pleasantries as far as the corner, the subway or a cab, you leave them with an image of yourself as *one of them*. Instead of the idea that you're there, *still* there, simply for the free drinks, which may lead them to question your motivation for showing up at all. Like dress, drink selection and decorum, when you're out with a group, an awareness of timing is key to the overall dynamic.

DON'T DIE ON THE WAY HOME.

It's simple. Don't drink and drive.

CHAPTER SIX

EVENTS

New York events can build you or break you. Entertaining in this city requires a deft hand, creative thinking, and perfect timing. Events by their very nature are public affairs, a perfect occasion to advertise our cachet and mystique—or not. There is little quite so awkward as chatting up guests at your own bad party. Never mind one that clients have paid you to throw in their honor. Assiduous planning is required to make sure you're not sent back to Dogpatch, Idaho in a box.

An event is one of the single most powerful ways to recommend your client to the press and cognoscenti you need to reach. Planning an event automatically gives you something with which to reach out to editors and reporters. If you play your cards right, it is news in and of itself.

Events generate effective buzz. Bringing groups together to show support for a cause or celebrate a debut establishes communication between large numbers of people simultaneously. At the heart of every event is a community whose very presence implies that they are open to receiving your message. If you pull it off *well,* you vastly amplify that message by exploiting the chic set's desire to be seen in the right place at the right time. And that means good press.

And that's a big "if".

Smooth logistics, orchestration and protocol define the success—or failure—of any event. Great events don't just happen. You can't put one together overnight. It takes weeks, even months, to plan an affair that will draw the crowd you want and send them away so dazzled by the experience that you get the ink you're hoping for.

Just coming up with a concept that works requires more than simply leaping up, crying "Let's put on a show!" and drawing up a guest list of those you'd like to impress. It takes thoughtful preparation, genuine intelligence, sharp instincts, imagination, hard work and a solid grasp of the context. And sometimes all that effort and ingenuity can still blow up in your face.

Once the message and strategy are fleshed out, your work has barely begun. If not you, then people you absolutely trust must control every detail of planning, provisions and decor, transportation, invitations, guest considerations, and programming. An oversight anywhere can result in worse publicity than you would have earned by doing nothing at all.

DON'T
STAGE AN EVENT FOR
ITS OWN SAKE.

This may have been a charming sentiment in your dorm room days, but it isn't going to pass muster in publicity. The first question any experienced publicist asks is, "To what end?" If you don't have an answer for that beyond "fun", you need to consider a career not in publicity, but in event planning or hospitality management. Those fine trades both rest on the presumption you're making: that someone else has a rationale for the event and your sole task is simply to make it happen. Of course, people of that stripe will be tremendously useful to you as a publicist, but in this profession events are necessitated for purposes it will be *your* job to define.

Events require tremendous effort to pull off properly. More importantly, they're not always the best way to achieve your goals as a publicist. Ones that are mismatched to the purpose, ill timed or half-assed merely create a grander stage on which to fail.

Events only make (good) sense provided that *a)* there's a concrete message or piece of news to relay; *b)* the event highlights a client's product or service; *c)* you or your client are sufficiently well-known that the (right) people will naturally want to attend.

Opening a new location is a good justification, launching a new brand or product line even better. A client who has already enjoyed some press may supply enough juice to attract the caliber of editors you need. With all those factors in play at once, *maybe* it's time to party.

DON'T BASK IN SECONDHAND LIMELIGHT.

Oscar Night. The glamour. The fashion. The celebrity. What could be a greater opportunity for the well-oiled publicity machine to ride a red carpet to victory? How about Sundance? The Grammys? Cannes!

How about your client?

Subordinating your event to some external context primarily affirms the importance of that context at the expense of your client's endeavor. There are times when auxiliary events can lend weight to yours, but they mustn't become the focus. For example, when an event is the news cycle (i.e. Sundance), and your client is part of the process, then it makes sense to attract the pool of press tasked with covering it.

Below is an example of a release inviting press to an event at Sundance.

INDEPENDENCE IN FILM.
INDEPENDENCE IN INVESTING.
(Sundance Gives a Glimpse of Successful New Film Investment Model)

(Park City, Utah)–The most compelling story this year at Sundance may just be outside of the competition.

IndieVest, the film financier, distributor, and production studio is screening exclusive behind-the-scenes footage on January 16th and 17th for IndieVest Executive Producers of their first film, *St. John of Las Vegas*, starring Steve Buscemi, Sarah Silverman, and Romany Malco. (The film will be released nationally during 2009.)

SJLV was completely funded by IndieVest members making investments directly or through wealth management firms. The company has created the first managed-risk platform for investing in independent films. IndieVest guarantees distribution of its films through industry connections and will not begin production on a project without 100% of the production and distribution funds in hand. Achieving both of those goals is usually the major hurdle for production companies.

An IndieVest member gets access to a database of top-tier projects IndieVest has in the works, selects those of interest and is involved in the entire process of the film's creation and distribution (this includes trips to the production set, an invitation to the world premiere, and a film credit of IndieVest Executive Producer, among other consideration).

"By solving the most significant and persistent market challenges, IndieVest makes becoming an IndieVest Executive Producer of independent films an alternative investment that even the most prudent and discerning investors can enjoy," says Wade Bradley, founder and CEO of IndieVest.

And unlike other alternative investment markets which may exuberantly bubble, then burst—like the art, energy and Real Estate markets of late—the film industry remains resolute, and moves counter to bad economic times.

According to *Variety*, which recently published box office business for the past year, ticket sales for 2008 clocked in at $9.63 billion, ahead of the $9.62 billion earned in 2007. Admissions were down roughly 4%, far less than declines in other sectors of the economy.

"People understand that entertainment is going to out-perform the rest of the market during a recession," comments Bradley. "They're looking at entertainment as a safe haven."

For interview opportunities with IndieVest <www.indievest.com> and select members during Sundance, please contact PUBLIC at 212.431.1470.

What: Behind-the-scenes screening, dinner, and cocktail party
When: Jan 16th, 17th at 7:30pm
Where: IndieVest Lounge, Hotel Park City

An after party can come off like an afterthought—unless it is chock-full of notable people and poised for the social pages.

Audiovisual razzle-dazzle is not what you're looking for. Glamorous events like those you'll occasionally stage tend to earn the notice of *print* publications. Avoid going up against too much competition for magazine space and editor time by paying studious attention to current events and the publishing industry's calendar. Hold your event at a time of day that is convenient and makes a statement: daytime for something more casual, evening for anything more serious or formal.

Events can be fantastic for targeting short and long lead publications. Pitch monthly and quarterly magazines, fashion books and newspaper lifestyle sections. Be sure you have a product or service the press will benefit from in a brand that will interest a wide readership. Understand an editor's interests or risk appearing oblivious to their content.

Once all the foregoing checks out, an event becomes a tremendously influential tool, one that is most suitable when the information you have is more efficiently disseminated en masse than through one-on-one meetings. Having a number of editors attending to your client's message at once instantly multiplies the enthusiasm for that message by the number of editors present. As they jockey to position your story, in fact, the sum of exposure can even become greater than its parts.

And that's limelight you can call your own.

DON'T
KILL A GREAT EVENT
WITH TERRIBLE
TIMING.

Another firm we know too, too well was representing a fashion brand with an impressive new store in the works. Dedicated to the idea of making a splash in the media, they had limited contacts in the New York fashion community and were hell bent on a party. Smack in the middle of Fashion Week. Only the busiest time of year for Manhattan style editors. Only the most competitive environment for any label looking to attract guests to an event.

The product was good, but not alluring enough in a seven-day avalanche of major names from Marc Jacobs to Marchesa.

However, the brand's creator had an unrealistic sense of the interest her product would arouse in discriminating fashion editors during their most over-extended week. It was designated for the "plus size" market, a hard sell with style journalists, who rarely give a nod line to anything in the double digits at the best of times.

Our heroes pled, even begged, to move the event date to anything *but* Fashion Week, when they might find a more optimal date and an open ear from these editors. The company insisted on moving forward. They ultimately settled on a daytime, Saturday champagne brunch unchallenged by key events.

But what fashion editor is dragging herself out of bed before 9:00 am after a crazy week of day-and-night fashion events, when she's 100% been at a fab FW *fête* the night before the Saturday brunch? That event is dead before the stamps are licked. Unless Valentino is hosting, no one is showing up.

Saturday. Fashion Week. Lukewarm product. Rain. Bad.

What the client wasn't getting was what Fashion Week means to editors. Before them spreads one of the year's great panoplies, pulling them in many directions. With numerous major events scheduled concurrently, they must decide which of the season's key collections they can afford to miss, not which of no immediate importance to add in.

Anyone hoping to attract editors to an event must therefore be mindful of scheduling it both on the calendar and in the daybook so as not to conflict even remotely with anything of greater status. Editors will simply choose the more relevant event. Period.

DON'T INCONVENIENCE YOUR GUESTS (OR WORSE YET, BORE THEM).

Lots of things can ruin an event. Like a remote location that editors won't go out of their way to get to.

Of course, unusual spaces can be highly effective. Stylish private residences are almost irresistible. Boats, parks, museums... I've even seen memorable—and tasteful—events held in sex shops. Chic ones, of course. New York also has plenty of great conventional venues such as restaurants, event spaces, and your clients' own retail spaces, if appropriate.

Hotels are excellent. Everything is right there, and many are close to Midtown, thus convenient from anywhere in Manhattan. Fold press into the event, and you can even negotiate on rates. Hotels love exposure, too.

DON'T
PUT YOUR FOOT
IN THAT.

Now it's my turn to tell on myself, as major disasters have the potential to breed great experiences. I am generally ambitious when it comes to idea execution. A client of mine had strong connections in Aspen, and we strategized a GRAND event at the top of Aspen Mountain. For the gala opening of a new $30M club and restaurant, we would shuttle well-heeled celebs and locals up and down the mountain on the gondola. Brilliant, right? Yes, in theory.

After investing tens of thousands of dollars of my client's money and courting the proper charities and Aspenites, opening night was cancelled at the last minute by the owners. Chatter had reached them about this event being "too glitzy" for a restaurant housed in the same space as one once adored by all in town.

Point being that in all my due diligence and recon, I neglected to consider what the community was thinking. I was a bull in a china store, paying attention to only one facet of the Aspen continuum. In the end, this injured my client's bottom line—and my own reputation.

On the bright side, we brought Sasha and Digweed from London to perform privately for a handful of guests at the St. Regis (awesome, by the way). Clearly, I spent all my time plying my clients with drinks, food, positive attention, and piles of swag…

What I learned is to do my homework on venue and theme. Laugh away, kids. Your time will come.

Always consider relevance. Novel locations must make sense in relation to your product or service. What are your goals for the event itself? Why have you chosen this backdrop?

And budget. Only a spectacularly wealthy client can afford a spectacularly opulent event. A $40 million estate in Georgica Pond might make a gorgeous setting for your industry luncheon, but if your client can't swing the rental, neither can you.

Offsetting my misread of Aspen's community, I did get one thing right with the event: the wow factor. It's important, and don't downplay the ambition.

Try things.

DON'T
FORGET TO SEND THE
INVITATIONS!

So where is everybody? You've arranged a lovely and, if you must say so yourself, truly unique event space, spared no expense on decor, lined up a musical act to die for. Why the hell hasn't anybody shown up yet besides two guys from the third rate weekly who got here 15 minutes early to ravage the buffet?

Maybe those e-mails you sent out last week went straight to people's spam or something?

It may seem unlikely that anyone would plan an event but leave out the detail essential to having anyone attend. However, I've seen stranger things.

My point is that without invitations—and surpassingly engaging ones at that—you may as well have no event at all. Clearly, without an invitation nobody knows they're invited, but some of an invitation's other, equally important functions are less tangible.

The character of your event is encapsulated in this first touch. Treat the invitations as the marketing tool that they are. They must convey a clear message without being overbearing or trite. The best ones are elegant yet striking, express the theme, purpose and tenor of the occasion, and inspire the recipient to attend.

Don't shy away from spending a seemingly inordinate sum on this all-important first impression. Invitations announce your intent. Give scrupulous attention to their tone and design.

DON'T LEAVE THE DEVIL IN THE DETAILS.

An event is the sum of a million moving parts, most of them costly, each of them interacting with others at crucial moments and any of them thus capable of bringing all the others down. Invitations, staff, sponsorships, food and drinks, transport, security, guest list, photo ops, VIPs, media, talent, permits, music, lighting, decor: lose sight or control of one and watch the others unravel in turn.

Organization is paramount. You cannot bring this off without a team, and it is imperative that staff be organized with a disciplined chain of command, a clear delegation of responsibilities, and minimal ego.

Avoid working with people you aren't 100% certain you can depend on, and start as far in advance as you possibly can. Plan regular meetings at each level to track progress as well as identify and monitor issues. Preparation depends on forethought, communication and meticulous scheduling.

Event Timeline

6 MONTHS PREVIOUS
—Assess the goals of the event
—Check potential event timing with editorial calendars, holiday calendars, and local event calendars
—Outline budgetary constraints
—Brainstorm concepts for event
—Start scouting locations

3 MONTHS PREVIOUS
—Put together invitation
—Pick location
—Start considering guest and press lists
—Select photographers (if needed)
—Decide on and book entertainment

1 MONTH PREVIOUS
—Have solidify concept of event details
—Select and make firm agreements with vendors (food, decor, etc.)

—Confirm that client is fully on board re: goals, details, and budget for event
—Send invitations to complete guest list

1 WEEK PREVIOUS
—Aggressively pursue RSVPs—call, call, *call* on the phone!

DAY OF
—Have guest list doubly confirmed
—Clearly delineate and delegate responsibilities
—Establish concrete schedule for the entire proceedings (and be prepared to adapt in the face of the unexpected)
—Create separate press list, and set up all known interviews with sources
—Smile!

DAY AFTER
—Sleep in
—Document all needed follow-up and next steps from press interactions
—Send "Thank You" letters

DON'T
GET SNARKED.

Guests are smart, of course. They *are* capable of figuring things out on their own: how to get to the location from their office or what kind of shoes to wear for an outdoor event in a partially wooded area. How long in advance to RSVP or what "dressy casual" means.

But do you actually want to leave *any* particular group—with its predictable share of sartorially inventive and directionally challenged, picky, tardy, even snarky, and sensible-shoe-adverse members—to its own devices? If I didn't have the good sense to bring proper footwear to your resort promotion on the beach, and I'm the one wielding the nation's acid pen, who's going to end up looking foolish: the journalist walking away in $400 loafers filled with sand or the publicist who didn't remind guests to consider their footwear?

The best precaution, one that speaks to your competence, is to organize guests down to the finest detail.

Primarily, you need to ensure that the people you are throwing this event for show up. Mail invitations well in advance. Follow up by phone on your RSVP deadline, whether they RSVP or not (very few will bother).

Organize your guest list. Seating is an art form; place people in the company of those they will enjoy. Program the event so that they encounter each other as soon as possible after arriving. No one should be left to feel marginalized or disengaged.

Finally, almost as crucially as finessing the invitation, make professional livery service available to all who request it. Confirm when and where it will pick them up, and provide those who decline it with clear, detailed directions.

DON'T
FLUB.

It does you no good to assemble a dynamic crowd if they go away unsure what it was they were meant to be excited about.

A muddled, lackluster announcement delivered without props or visuals; a featured service not demonstrated or conceptualized; above all a consumer product not on hand, dramatically displayed and, if appropriate, available to sample: slapdash messaging will result in far less coverage, with far less emphasis, than it could have or your client had hoped for.

What are you *demonstrating* to the members of the press in attendance? Is this a fashion show? In what manner are the clothes being presented? A new line of vodka? How is it being served? Regardless what you're promoting, make sure that you have something concrete to display to the editors, that it is displayed appealingly—that the message is unmistakable.

The same level of creativity needs to go into introducing, displaying and demonstrating your product, service or news. Where are you setting up displays, how and when will you reveal them, and how should they be designed? What is the relationship between your message and the samples or gifts being distributed at the event? What is the program? How are you keeping the party in a comfortable state of flow so that everyone invited receives the benefit of your preparations?

Considerations like these, which underscore the reason for holding an event, will demand more wit and imagination than almost any other part of your job.

If they aren't among your most rewarding challenges, question why it is that you want to be a publicist in the first place.

DON'T
FAIL TO ENTERTAIN.

So, your invitations were winning. The event was rendered flawlessly: organized staff, glittering guests, an enchanting location; your client's message impressive, the swag resplendent. Why, then, such a perfunctory tone to the thank yous?

No matter how astounding a presentation you've made, the extent to which you've gratified your editors on a visceral level will reflect in how positively they are disposed to treat your product. Everyone must leave happy—not happily. While your primary job is to advance your clients' business, you must be driven by passion, creativity, quality and taste.

The essentials are food, expertly prepared in generous quantities for refined palates; cocktails, ditto; sophisticated music or entertainment, a dynamic space, good lighting, and lots of stylish people from a range of milieus.

Don't shy from mixing in some fabulous non-media types. The media crowd attends the same roster events all the time; a few social wild cards and random beauties keep things interesting. You want to be known for throwing *enjoyable* events, ones that editors will attend no matter what you're flogging—and 7/10ths of that is vibe.

CHAPTER SEVEN

COACHING YOUR CLIENTS

Media training is essential for your clients.

Among your most important skills as a publicist is an ability to command, even manipulate, the flow of information from the client to the media, and from the media to the consumer.

Teaching your clients to come across in the most effective and persuasive manner is crucial; the more personally winning and professionally relevant they appear, the more frequent and desirable their placements will be. At the same time, presenting editors and producers with a well-rounded punter and an on-point pitch shows respect for their priorities. While successfully advancing your client, a proposal that's concise, on message and doesn't waste time also reinforces your relationships with valuable media contacts.

Though the two require equal savvy, there are inherent distinctions between print and broadcast outlets.

My good friend and colleague, Sean Kevelighan (VP Media Relations North America, Zurich Financial Services Group) has spent over 10 years in Capitol Hill public policy—from big agency life to the White House. He is especially attuned to the importance of understanding the other side of the media. That is, our side of the media, and what we need to understand to prepare best for an interview.

As a seasoned expert in the field, Sean emphasizes the importance of understanding your audience. The media is not your friend, but neither is it your enemy. You both need each other; viewing yourself either as at odds with the media *or* as their partner often can actually get in the way of accomplishing your goals.

The media, respectfully put, view themselves as the Fourth Estate (the other three being Church, State, and Citizenry). This means they take their job as civil servants and stewards of the public good very seriously, and expect to be treated as such.

Just like you and me, journalists feel ambition. Strong ambition. When you combine this with the concept of public stewardship, you have a highly motivated correspondent whose job and philosophy is to get useful news. Reporters want to be a part of coverage that provides value, education, and interest to their public, but they also want to be the first to break a story, and they want the story to be big, achieving these ends at times through subtlety, misdirection and inventive interview tactics.

Ultimately, every member of the media wants access to information. Your attempts to appeal to them on any other terrain will play as false or, worse, pointless.

Broadcast has the quality of performance. Therefore, appearance and attitude are at a premium, sometimes even at the expense of what is actually being said. The founder of an inspired, new high-end brand, so eager to pitch her concept that she over-explains, speaks too quickly, is unclear, breaks a sweat, or in any way loses her composure, does a disservice to her business, regardless of how innovative her brand may be.

She's no advertisement for your talent either, but whose fault is that?

Before letting clients near anyone with a microphone, make sure they're prepared for the spotlight. That they are capable of delivering sound bites with measured cadence, varied inflection and naturalistic poise; will arrive well groomed and well dressed; sit up straight, look interviewers in the eye, refrain from waving their hands around or unconsciously fussing with their hair.

Perhaps you think these TV producers are a little presumptuous, getting an entire spot without lifting a finger and then expecting your client to be both engaging and self-effacing.

First, to grasp the finer points of TV fully, you'll need a working understanding of the machinations of broadcast media. Overseeing a continuous flow of guests, media handlers, and story topics, Hayley Herst, an Executive Producer for FOX Television, offers the following list of broadcast absolutes. Commit this expert advice to memory.

Before escorting clients to a television interview, a publicist who was truly first-class would instruct them as follows.

1. **KNOW YOUR TOPIC.** Write down bullet points on a 3 x 5 card and keep it with you. You want to stay on point and get your message across.

2. **INFORM THE PRODUCER AHEAD OF TIME WHAT YOU WANT TO TOUCH UPON.** If producers know what you can talk about then they can frame questions accordingly; you won't be caught off guard by questions you aren't prepared to answer.

3. **ALWAYS SIT THREE QUARTERS TO THE CAMERA WITHOUT LOOKING STRAIGHT INTO IT.** Make sure you are looking at the anchor who is asking you the question. If you angle yourself slightly on the chair then you won't give a profile shot

to the camera, and we'll still be able to see your face.

4. KEEP YOUR ANSWERS AS BRIEF AS POSSIBLE. Going off on tangents or too deeply into detail just gets viewers lost and takes up precious air time you could devote to your core message.

5. THINK VISUALLY. TV is all about the visual element. If you have visual aides that help get your point across, bring them. A straight interview can get boring if you don't have things to show what you are talking about.

Print, on the other hand, is more relaxed in many ways. The anxiety of performance is not there; interviews may be conducted over coffee, lunch, or drinks, in your office, in some charming restaurant, or entirely over the phone. But don't be lulled by this seemingly looser atmosphere; there are rules. Overlooking them, or allowing your client to, can cost you the editorial you're being paid to deliver.

You may find it odd that print journalists call at random moments with oddly assorted questions, rather than simply inviting your client to talk face to face. This is because, in many cases, they'd rather not make time for what they view as "the whole dog and pony show", particularly for one-page mentions or less. So they've framed the story together from facts you've provided in a written press release and are now simply filling in the blanks as they finalize copy.

To finesse this sort of interaction, answer queries promptly–the writer may be on deadline–and provide exclusive quotes via email, requested or not. Depending on your client, this isn't always the worst-case scenario, as remarks can be pre-polished prior to sending. Journalists are far more likely to incorporate these comments if rather than dryly reiterating known information they contain wit, personality, or speak to an angle that cannot be lifted out of the press release as winningly.

Unless you feed them a line from your client that reads more appealingly in the first person, journalists will recast the information in their own, better words, and you'll lose a valuable opportunity to have a client quoted "directly" in a story penned by a writer who won't make time for a real interview.

Much of this chapter speaks to broadcast as well as print. Not having the facts straight can be as much of a setback on live air as in a magazine interview. Smart dress and demeanor are crucial to television but offer an advantage in print, too. Overall, to win frequent, widespread placements along with the respect of your clients and media contacts, it helps to follow a few essential guidelines.

DON'T
EXPECT THE MEDIA
TO SHARE YOUR
CLIENT'S AGENDA.

Bottom line: your client is here to sell a product. It may be a fine one, beautifully produced to the most exacting standards. But at the end of the day it's still just a product, and most clients have no idea what the media want to hear.

They aggrandize themselves, present their business with inflated rhetoric, fall back on canned marketing messages, use grandiose jargon, and generally make the mistake that their 15 minutes in the spotlight is all about *them*.

This is why they need *you*.

The media is selling something of its own: content. Your expert marketing acumen and networking skills allow clients an opportunity to supply some of that content. What holds that matrix together is credibility. The moment clients start to pitch themselves, become intoxicated with *personal* publicity or otherwise confuse the message, they cease to be genuinely marketable, losing their spot on the roster and quite possibly your future access to valued media contacts. The inadequately coached client can be an expensive prospect all round.

Encapsulating the many factors that make their product essential, not squandering their fifteen minutes basking in the limelight, your clients draw credibility directly from their ability to place a service or item within a wider context.

To establish an idea successfully as being timely and worthwhile, a client must be able to highlight the standards, technology, craft or expertise that make it *particularly* useful while deftly relating it to the preferences, needs and lifestyle of a target market.

Effective publicity wins the trust of consumer markets and the media while increasing a client's visibility. Once those goals have been achieved, less pitching is required.

DON'T
EXPECT THE PUBLIC
TO, EITHER.

Having misperceived the media's agenda and chafed journalists with egocentric claptrap, the second blunder *that* client will often make is to bore the public with minutiae. It's natural. Instead of ingratiating themselves with producers, editors and reporters while schmoozing the media, your clients are primarily occupied making their case to the bankers, investors and partners who keep their lights turned on.

It's only natural they should default to the investor pitch, marketing copy, or "branded" chitchat. Don't let them. The more dexterous your clients are with their own product or service knowledge, the better your interview—as long as their knowledge is relevant. Meaning: memorized bullet points suck.

Promotional language has its place:
in promotions.

And not to disparage the American intellect, but the broadcast standard is to relay information at an easily digestible level. Occasions focused on publicity should find your client delivering a message that's clear and engaging to the consumer within the context of a media-friendly storyline, not one aimed at recruiting equity partners.

Prepare clients to move from the general to the specific. Lead with the information that fits the product, service or event into the largest possible picture, broad strokes that highlight angles pertinent to the most viewers. Then fill in successive layers of detail.

A benefit for rainforest conservation, for example, will be lost in a deluge of detail if its spokesperson launches directly into biodiversity profiles and an analysis of international response. Focus audience attention on information relevant to the event itself first; then move on to facts related to the cause.

Save the forest despite the trees.

DON'T FORGET TO REPEAT YOURSELF.

(As told by Sean Kevelighan)
The art of good messaging is more refined than simply engaging in a comfortable conversation with an interviewer. If you enter into a media situation with this in mind you might appear

at ease, confident, and well informed, but you won't be 100% effective.

A conversation's natural flow is loosely tied to a question-and-answer format, and this is the structure that almost everyone expects when interacting with the media. But if you simply answer every question the reporter asks, no matter how deftly, the only person getting everything they want from the interview is the reporter.

People who act as excellent sources to the media all learn the art of pivoting. We've already covered how loathsome reporters (and audiences) find canned messaging, but here's where a touch of that can come in handy, if skillfully incorporated: change the flow of the conversation to question, short answer, and quick pivot back to already established messaging.

When done correctly, this is a seamless way of ensuring that the reporters aren't the only ones getting what they want.

Bottom Line:
  QUESTION > ANSWER
  —Reporters get what they want
  QUESTION > ANSWER + MESSAGE
  —Reporters get what you both want

DON'T
GO IN COLD.

Striding across a vast, buffed expanse of marble, you and your client present yourselves at a granite security desk the size of a Bentley. The elevator glides upward until its doors open onto a luxe reception area dominated by that logo you see every time you turn on the news. It's not actually swooping toward you this time; it just feels like it.

(Oh! If only you'd gone over those talking points with your client!)

To be presented as a valid source of information—to earn a story the media—clients must be prepped beforehand. Period. They must be equipped with readily available contacts and information. Placements result from a client, fully briefed on the big picture, with a facility for relating it to the media's specific interests.

Print interviews are more probing than TV. The format allows journalists to stop, think, review and double check stories before they run. Print media reveals inconsistencies and gaffes more glaringly than broadcast. The reporter has spent more time researching the topic—and your client—than someone under deadline for an a.m.

television show. On which note, it is handy to know that magazines, which have longer lead times as well as fact checking departments, will ferret out more discrepancies than newspapers. And of the English-language media, American magazines are far more disposed to fact check than those based in the U.K.

In any case, make sure your client is suitably briefed. If needed, rehearse. Do what it takes. Know who the reporter, editor or producer is. How the publication or program views the story. Understand what they want from your client. Define the facts and phrases that should be emphasized so they make it into the final cut.

Briefing documents are invaluable to your client's success.

DON'T
LET YOUR CLIENT
LOSE FOCUS.

So your client and the newscaster are chatting away, getting on famously. Everything is going swimmingly... until Barb drops an oblique, unmistakably snide reference to a certain key competitor...

... and a huge Red Alert to you.

Remember, the average attention span, around 15 minutes on a single topic, shortens dramatically under stress—people misinterpret each other and botch facts. Second, live TV doesn't give "take-backs".

Joe Biden is famous for his for excruciating gaffes, but while the White House dream team can almost always spin out of harm's way, you may not fare so well.

Make sure clients go into any interview informed enough to follow tangents but practiced enough to maintain the story's goal: your core agenda. Build their confidence and sharpen their reflexes. Drill them backward, forward and upside down on the three or four key messages you don't want them to miss. Furthermore, clients must be able to address sensitive topics, even when led by the interviewer, with aplomb. Refer to adversaries or adversities with magnanimity and tact, sidestepping negativity, deftly avoiding the precarious, always assuming the mic is on and never assuming any comment is "off the record". As nonprofessionals, chances are your clients will offer the media enough creative temptation that you can do nothing about. Forestall the missteps you can.

After all, who's editing the tape?

DON'T
FORGET TO ACT.

Body language can be as much of a cue as verbal communication. If it signals confidence, particularly in a challenging interview, you win. If it underscores reticence or nervousness, you lose. It can be that simple. In broadcast performance is essential, so a confident façade is an enormous asset. Audiences need to respect, trust, and ideally admire your client.

Poor presentation can give the impression of vacuity, insincerity, even fraudulence—an all-too-convenient hook for anyone looking to hang you on it. If you let this happen to your clients you won't be asked back, and the 10 million viewers who saw them tank won't look kindly on the message.

Some stumbles are unavoidable. Most are preventable. There are, for example, elegant ways to say, "I've no idea". Unable to answer a question, a client may come out ahead by deferring to a reliable source. Anticipate trouble spots prior to the interview, and arm your client with options in case they crop up.

DON'T WEAR WHITE.

Then there's physical appearance.

White "blows out" on camera. Don't wear it. Avoid patterns, too; they may look great in person, but they unsettle television pixels in unsightly ways. Stick with basic colors instead, even for print.

An attractive appearance enhances a clients' credibility—even if their expertise is limited. This means that the character-themed tie your client proudly purchased in Orlando to wear on his first CNN appearance should be, um, burned.

DON'T LET THEM STARE LIKE A DEER IN HEADLIGHTS.

Only the most experienced professional performer moves seamlessly between the lens and other personalities on screen. To achieve this "naturalism", clients must be aware of the camera but never look into it. Their gaze should move between the interviewer, any fellow guests, and whatever props or objects are on hand. Cameras, microphones, ear-buds, and on set staff: as if nonexistent.

Your client may have an amazing background in wine, but looking blankly into the camera simply shows viewers someone acting awkwardly with Meredith Vieira. When what they should see is a couple of people chatting pleasantly on an engaging topic, oblivious to anyone's presence but their own.

DON'T
LET THEM THROW UP
ON FOX NEWS.

I once had an overzealous client on deck for live remote with FOX News, set to broadcast from our location throughout the day beginning at 7 a.m. Suffering from nerves amplified by caffeine addiction, my chain-smoking client was over-amped and over-stimulated. Thirty seconds before his live interview, he became nauseous after his ear mic was inserted and disturbed his equilibrium.

With the producers freaking as their "expert" fled off camera to hurl, I found myself screaming at him like a high school football coach: *Drink some water, man up and get your ass on camera!* It worked, thankfully.

Point being, it was largely my fault. I should have been serving the guy wheat grass and OJ, not lighting his cigarette and ordering more lattes. To perform at their best, it's paramount for your clients to focus on optimum health before any segment: getting enough sleep; drinking plenty of water, moderating caffeine intake, and, I can assure you, avoiding heavy meals.

DON'T PISS OFF THE CONDÉ NASTIES.

They're called that for a reason, especially in the realms of beauty, fashion and lifestyle. A single affront can very easily be your last shot at an entire publication. When accompanying a client to the New York Times building or Hearst Publications, be on time, keep visitor badges in inside pockets, not slapped on like a couple of conventioneers, and dress impeccably. Be sharp. Be alert. Have your facts together.

Most importantly, respect deadlines. Yes, the story comes out months from now and this crowd does seem chattily laissez-faire. But when it comes down to the wire, you still haven't submitted a client's bio or company profile, and an editor has to point these facts out, moods change quickly.

The magazine writers' more freeform approach gives you no license to relax your own standards. Perhaps you've never met face-to-face with the reporter and are, in fact, lounging at home in your knickers while bandying his questions about. You must nonetheless conduct the conversation as if having it over lunch on his tab at Acquavit.

DON'T
FINESSE A PRINT
REPORTER.

Nobody smells blood in the water like an eager, young reporter. One thing always to remember is that reporters, much like you, are ambitious. They are hungry to break interesting news and would rather have a story than your friendship.

So, save *your* time (or better, your credibility) by understanding the value of *their* time and getting to the point. Newspapers have faster deadlines than any other media outlet, and their writers can dispense with the pleasantries. This is not to say that courtesy should be sacrificed, but excessive gestures of kindness should be left at the doors of the New York *Times*.

Don't send gifts. Don't bring freebies. And don't hang your hopes of a solid story on a wink and a smile.

CHAPTER EIGHT

CULTURAL LITERACY

Powerbrokers, influencers, and icons—their occasional populist affectations notwithstanding—are found in greatest number among the cultured elite. If you can't tell a Viogner from a Cabernet, Don Imus may appreciate your support, but don't expect even him to tarry in your booth at Sardi's. More importantly than these people's attention you will need their *respectful* attention. You'll get that most reliably by speaking their actual language—not just the one with which they amuse their public.

The one fact I've hoped most to demonstrate to you throughout this book is that, as a publicist dealing with the cognoscenti of our aesthetic, social and political life, you will find sophistication in matters of comportment, taste and intellect not optional to your work, but essential. More than a few of your editors, producers and writers hold their task on par with that of the serious artists, authors and thinkers of their age; cultural mastery is nothing less than these people's professional *raison d'être*.

Knowing this, and simply knowing New York City, you must work to attain a cultural vocabulary. Cultural literacy does not consist in memorizing some hallowed list of names, events, works, and movements. Rather, it is something you can only truly understand by pursuing it as a lifestyle.

New York City is, by far, the best place in the world to study humanity, no comparison. People, places, art, theatre, dining, writing, dance, even just perambulating: culturally, New York City is a consummate garden, quite simply the best place to cultivate the senses in harmony with the mind. It should then be no surprise that this is the city where cultural awareness also counts most. When you first move here it can be daunting to assimilate to *any* circle, much less a highly cultured one; nonetheless, earning acceptance to the latter will prove forever valuable.

A dear friend of mine, Aaron Alden (owner of the renowned production house Robot Repair), gave me such sanctuary when I first moved here. He said without reservation that it takes three years to settle into New York City's rhythm. And after ten years, I still feel like there is impressive room to grow in new cultural directions.

ABT's new *prima ballerina*... What's opening at the Met... The Central Park Conservancy's upcoming season... You may not be ready to assert yourself in these conversations, but take the opportunity to listen. Seriously. Later, investigate. To acquire cultural terminology, concepts, and eventually opinions takes less brilliance than time. As well as a little devotion. Breadth is thin without detail, while depth is tedious without variety. Seek both with ardor.

Edification may not instantly gratify, of course. My older brother used to hammer me with the order to "accept the burden of thought", truly words to live by. To refine your interests and investigate unfamiliar subjects requires persistence over time. So when *Weekend At Bernie's II* starts singing its Siren's song while *The Forsythe Saga* gathers dust on the nightstand, remind yourself of the opportunities you can create only through continued growth.

Meanwhile, read on.

DON'T
BEHAVE LIKE A
PHILISTINE.

"I just saw the Pollock retrospective at the Modern, and it was an absolute feast," your arts and entertainment editor gushes. "Have you been yet?"

Maybe you couldn't tell a pollock from a halibut. Maybe you think any eight-year-old could do a better picture than these abstract so-called artists. Maybe you'd just as soon be out at the lanes with a pitcher and a pack of Marlboro Lights.

Despite the film of sweat that appears on your upper lip when anyone mentions a bit of culture you haven't encountered or can't comprehend, they generally aren't trying to make you look dumb. As a rule, they're actually expressing genuine enthusiasm for the subject, and any eye-rolling, groaning and snorting on your part is guaranteed not only to look like a flimsy cover for your own insecurity, but to slight someone's feelings a little in the process. And that's no way to establish a fulfilling and mutually beneficial business relationship.

Rather than mumbling sheepishly, why not try taking an actual interest? What, after all, is it that has made your interlocutor so excited about her experience? If you've heard of the painter Jackson Pollock or perhaps even seen ads for the show, you might ask some questions based on that knowledge; if you still aren't sure why they've got fish at an art museum, your questions can be general enough to help you at least figure out what the conversation is about.

Who knows? You might just want to go check it out for yourself by the time you're done. And honesty: Wow! It's so refreshing if you have the personal fortitude for it.

Respect your and others' culture: people give of themselves to share it with you. Élan about some aspect of it is never out of place; contempt or disregard, always.

DON'T
NEGLECT THE FINER
PLEASURES.

Don't know much about history? ...biology? ...science book? ...French you took?

It may be a cute song, but in real life being devoid of intellectual curiosity or aesthetic interests just looks clueless. In a milieu that so thrives on this curiosity and interest, your listlessness is downright puzzling. Regardless of how you felt about your education (and not everyone you'll meet was an "A" student—yours truly chose several pass/fails), it's time to stop thinking of the more challenging cultural forms as a pedantic chore. The opera, the theater, the symphony, modern dance and ballet: the aura of "high" culture surrounding the traditional performing arts needn't deter you from, quite simply, buying yourself a ticket and going. Look at the listings in any newspaper, check out the titles online if you have to, and just go. There needn't be much more to it than that at first; just don't forget any points you might want to research later.

Should you attend the opera, which you should, I suggest learning about some aspect of the piece before you set out. Read the synopsis, study the time period, even the composer. You'll have an anchor to fasten to in a new environment, and I guarantee the experience will be an enriching one. If it isn't, well, you can always hit Times Square for a lap dance and a steak tartare at Flashdancers.

The visual arts in the vast sweep of their historical and geographic sources are represented perhaps nowhere else in the world as comprehensively as in New York. The bulk of the nation's most prestigious galleries and museums are all within a few miles of each other here, and admittance is often free. Just get there, and find something that catches your eye; audioguides and other resources will help you appreciate more fully what you're seeing.

And yes, the New York Public Library is also at your command. All you need to get your card is a bill or other official mail addressed to your name in any of the five boroughs. For a fuller understanding of any of the foregoing, or for browsing whatever might interest you (after all) in the humanities and social sciences, public life, the sciences and high technology, the library is, again, 100% free.

Don't know what the humanities and social sciences are? They've also got dictionaries for you.

DON'T
NEGLECT THE COMMON
PLEASURES, EITHER.

O.K., so you finally got out to the Wooster Group's new production last night. Still not sure what hit you, you're nonetheless exulting in the breeze atop your first cultural pinnacle. It sure as hell wasn't *Spamalot*, but you know, some of it actually seemed pretty cool. And now here comes your buddy. Triumphantly waving his brand new copy of *Grand Theft Auto XVIII*. After 20 hours camped outside some frigging mall in Weehauken. Fine. Don't be a snob. Just enjoy the game.

And wipe that sneer away, friend, before he notices!

If anything appeals less than obtuse disdain for the arts and letters, it's your correspondingly puerile disregard for the popular moment. Philistinism thinly masks a terror of cultural inadequacy. Yet snobbery conceals just as shabbily your sense of inferior popular consciousness.

And from the latter daily life gets its freshness each new decade, that cutting edge we'll smile back on ten years hence as charmingly *passé*.

Sports, entertainment, gadgets, fads, gossip and passing controversies constitute social glue. Look down your nose at pop culture, and you run the risk not only of condescending to someone you depend on every day, but of losing your media contacts' confidence that you understand and respect the passions of their audience (or their own obsession with *Star Wars* memorabilia).

Not to mention boring us all to death.

You really do have to know what's going on in the world. Who's getting attention? Over the next year or so, what's of interest to the rest of the world?

Still, like tequila shots at Chili's, pop culture is best partaken of responsibly.

Rather than watch every last episode of *Desperate Housewives* or pore over each page of *People* every month, use one of the many clip shows or news feeds to filter the information for you. Don't waste time and money slogging through inane detail when you can have someone else to do it free. That's what *they're* paid for, after all.

DON'T
READ THE *TIMES* FOR
GOSSIP OR THE *POST*
FOR CURRENT EVENTS.

Whichever of these papers you've been slavishly devouring every morning, it's time to break with timeworn habits and get some perspective. Oh, you don't read either one?

Then it's time to come out from under your rock.

Publicity, you see, depends on the public. If you have no clue what's going on in this realm, you won't be particularly effective at influencing it.

So let's talk cat people and dog people. Or Macs and PCs. *Times* readers consider the *Post* a borough-bound rag spewing hateful bilge upon the masses; *Post* readers think the *Times* a highfalutin, pink-o tract masquerading as objectivity.

For the record, I take the *Times*.

Yet you should understand what each paper provides. Simply and crudely, the *Times* authoritatively projects the educated perspective on current affairs through the lens of some of the world's finest journalistic minds. The *Post*, despite its braying populism and trite presentation, entertainingly furnishes—and shapes—workaday New York viewpoints through its local, sports and human interest stories. Its "Page Six" feature is one of America's most important sources of breaking celebrity gossip.

Other important publications include the *New Yorker*, not a font of current events, just a continual beacon of intellectual refinement; *Esquire* and *Vogue*, covering intellectual, social and political trends and figures thoughtfully but unpretentiously; and *Vanity Fair* for similar reasons.

Generally, reading remains the best means of reliably developing your mind while staying current. Use it! Read respectable, relevant news sources daily. Read good books—not necessarily always from the canon of "great" literature, but crafted with the erudition you would emulate. Seek higher perspectives.

An easy way to begin is to replace narrow, "fluffy" sources with more comprehensive substance. Replace "Page Six" on the subway with *The Economist* (the former is still fine for the john). Instead of your beloved morning shock-jocks, tune into NPR.

And actually listen.

DON'T
BEHAVE LIKE A BOOR.

We all know how tough New Yorkers are. They walk around ready for the slightest provocation. You need to be brusque, unflinching and unapologetic when dealing with them, yes? No, not really.

Don't you ever wonder why there aren't more fist fights?

Courtesy! Despite the stereotypes, in New York the exigencies of living in a big, crowded city have created a culture where every scrap of politeness carries double its weight. We are all crammed together on subway cars, struggling to get past slowpokes on the sidewalk, and competing for late-night cabs. In this environment, so much more loaded with stressors than your average suburb, taking the time to be nice to others literally makes the place livable.

Consider, too, that given the density of exceptionally powerful, intelligent people in New York City, here more than anywhere you have absolutely every incentive to be kind to your fellow man. That lard-ass you just cursed under your breath on the escalator could easily turn out to be none other than the national food editor to whose office you're running late. You know, the one to whom you were going to pitch your client's new organic cookbook? Regardless, the thought itself is classless.

Polite deference when entering cabs, trains and buildings is almost *de rigeur*. Mindfulness of protocol—who's doing a favor for whom—in introductions, greetings and farewells is a practice you'll notice more on display here than perhaps anywhere outside the society South. New Yorkers are also more likely to take note of your punctiliousness in expressing gratitude, good wishes and regards at appropriate times. Perhaps nowhere else is a random sneeze on the street as likely to be greeted with a chorus of "Bless you!"

Here, or in any other city that matters, interest, concern and engagement toward others are virtues matched only by reserve, deference and restraint toward yourself.

DON'T FORGET "PLEASE" AND "THANK YOU".

If you still step in front of people without so much as a nod... If you still take things handed to you and turn back to your task without acknowledgement... If you still blurt "what?" when you can't hear... Then prepare for slow progress.

Probably in New York or anywhere else.

Nobody—not your boss, not your client, not, really, your best friend—likes being taken for granted. In every generation oldsters can be heard to complain about the alarming decline in the manners of those coming after. Were every generation correct, by now we'd have devolved to boney-browed savages tearing at bloody carcasses for dinner.

Sure, different eras have viewed the social graces in more and less formally strict ways. But rather than a continual decline across generations, it's more likely that consciousness of such niceties within each generation increases as that generation matures.

In other words, grow up. This isn't beer pong anymore; it's life in New York City.

In business, relationships are the most priceless capital you have, and relationships are maintained through careful observance of other people's boundaries. As Robert Frost remarked, good fences make good neighbors.

He could as well have said the converse.

Whether sitting around the office, making appointments by phone or meeting with valued contacts, with any request the word "please" is likely appropriate, or at least indirect phrasing such as "would you" or "could you". When someone does something for you, however seemingly trivial, however preoccupied you may be, the words "thank you" indicate that you are aware of and appreciate the consideration. Likewise, when interrupting or intruding, "excuse me" requests permission and apologizes for inconvenience all at the same time. Can't hear me? Try "I beg your pardon".

I mention such absolute basics not because I think you were bred by wolves, but because in New York failure to observe them, even witnessed and not suffered directly, suggests you lack breeding at all.

DON'T
CHARGE DOWN THE
SIDEWALK LIKE A
MANIAC–OR BLUNDER
LIKE A TOURIST.

Yes, it sure is a big city. And yes, the trains sure are a mess. And yes! It sure is staggering how often one finds oneself in, well, staggering circumstances.

Welcome.

But please. Could you just let the rest of us onto the sidewalk? It need be neither a rampage nor a Sunday stroll. The former makes you look like a harried stiff from the boroughs, the latter like a hapless rube from parts even more remote.

Whether you're clenching your jaw, fixedly squeezing some gadget between your thumbs and caroming off the admins on Lexington, or waddling down Broadway gazing at the window ledges while people try to squeeze past, the one description that fits you least is "professional".

It's probably hard for many Manhattanites to say which annoys them more. Either is a hindrance and a hazard; neither will impress those you'd like to meet. Especially if they have the misfortune to accompany you.

Here are some simple rules of urban walking.

Move your ass out of the way to chat: moving crowds tend to divide into clusters of stationary and slower-moving people with quicker traffic between. If you have to take a call or converse with a companion, join the former.

No mall-walking: if there's enough space, walking side by side with one or two companions is pleasant. There usually isn't enough space. Pay attention.

No chicken, either: honestly. What are you going to do, fight some old babushka from Kiev? She'll whip your ass with that cart!

Say "excuse me" and "I beg your pardon": see above. Extra points if your client, superior or contact sees you do this.

Watch where you're going, not your freaking Blackberry: tonight's hookup won't be miffed if you take an extra 30 seconds to e-mail back. Otherwise, see above, do yourself a favor and "Move your ass out of the way..."

DON'T
FORGET WHICH FORK
IS WHICH. REALLY!

Guess what? Some of these people actually take the whole fork thing more or less as a given. Your graduation dinner humor won't save you now; in fact, it's only going to make everything still more awkward.

One of the first things you'll notice in cities like this is the semiconscious pride with which people take their dizzying array of restaurant choices for granted. For restaurateurs such variety means tremendous competition; even relatively modest establishments must pay strong attention to detail.

Which means you have a pretty good likelihood of encountering the fork thing.

Fortunately for you, it's simple. The one on the outside is for your salad. If there are three, the smallest is for desert. If you're still nervous, try Miss Manners or, better yet, that divine muse of American etiquette, Emily Post. Before you get to the restaurant.

More generally, you need to be aware of the expectations you'll usually confront in restaurants catering to a slightly (or much) better-heeled crowd, even at lunch. Business or well-assembled casual attire will put you most at ease. Show up looking like a slob (known in most of the country as "casual"), and I guarantee you'll feel like one. For guidance here, refer to my comments on attire and cocktails in previous chapters. This is also a good time to consider which seat is best so that you can offer it to a companion.

Looking over the wine list and menu, you'll realize that my earlier comments on drinking apply equally well to eating. Learn how to distinguish good food from mediocre; the knowledge will repay you for the rest of your life.

Always insist, no matter how feebly, on paying the check.

And *always,* always tip at least twenty percent! If the food or service was terrible, cut it to 15. If they pelted you with rocks and garbage, pocket change.

Nothing screams "hayseed" like a cheap restaurant patron.

DON'T
JUST SIT THERE
WHILE OTHERS PICK
UP YOUR TAB.

Remember what I said about "pleases" and "thank yous"? If you're sitting at lunch and your client or contact beats you to the check, you've lost a bit of face. If your media contact does, you may have lost more than that. If on top of this without a murmur you allow the other person to pay the tip as well, you're expressing inconsideration. Should they absolutely insist on paying the tab, accept graciously.

It's as simple as that.

These are people to whom you owe your livelihood, and who have put their faith in you sufficiently to extend that livelihood based on nothing other than your past performance, the reputation that precedes you and probably to no small degree the fact that they just like the cut of your jib. Don't treat them as if they owed you a handout on top of their business.

When getting into a cab, the person who gives the directions is generally the one who will pay the fare. Make sure that person is you. When together with a client or contact at a coat check or hotel check in, look for your chance to pay both tips. These are paltry sums, but it's the message you send by your willingness to pick up a tab that counts, not whether or how much you actually paid. Nor need you fear going broke playing the high roller you still aren't; others will most likely beat you to the check a good deal of the time.

And this is not to say that you should make a big scene. It's invariably painful to watch two people ceremonially tugging back and forth at a restaurant check. Don't go barging in front of companions while they're attempting to claim their wraps, either. Just look for your chance; that's all.

And when the other person does beat you to the punch, what do you say? (_____ !) Yes, you've got it...

DON'T
LIMIT YOUR
HORIZONS.

Pennsylvania to see my family. Puerto Rico to sit on the beach. Pennsylvania to see my family. Puerto Rico to sit on the beach. Orlando! Pennsylvania to see my family...

What a globe trotter. Are your hobbies as scintillating as your travels?

If your every break is invariably spent in one of two or three predictable ways, you're turning yourself into a potted plant. And not one that's very likely to bear great fruit. Your body and brain need variety. Constraining yourself to an unvarying seasonal routine dulls your mind, prevents your discovering new possibilities and worst, creates the kind of rut that clients and contacts can't help but feel themselves teetering on the edge of whenever they're around you.

So aside from sitting on the sofa dropping Pringles on your sweatshirt, what do you do with yourself when you aren't working?

My purpose in urging cultural pursuits on you at the beginning of this chapter was a practical one: to help you keep up intellectually with your professional environment. But the more effective you become as a publicist the less you can avoid shaping the culture around you. This makes you a member of the cultural elite, giving you a responsibility—and opportunity—to broaden your horizons constantly.

Ours is generally a world of technicians, intellectual equivalents of the couch potato engaged year after year in the same, narrow specialties. In contrast, I would have you aspire to the Renaissance ideal of 16th-Century Italian writer Baldesare Castiglione, who in his *Book of the Courtier* describes the ultimate, insider élite as someone with almost universal abilities. Through combined aptitude and study Castiglione's courtier masters everything from martial arts and sports, to writing and public speaking, to painting and dance.

Such universal mastery may be beyond any of our capacities in one lifetime, but working toward it gains you a flexibility that will serve your clients—and most importantly you—unsurpassably throughout your career.

CLOSING AND SPECIAL ACKNOWLEDGEMENTS

DON'T went through countless itera-
tions, beginning with my first attempt,
a scathing diatribe on the industry fitted with an uncomfortable number of
F*bombs and even more pompous language, in a voice that was downright
mean.

In fact, I offered the first drafts to new
employees on their first day (charming,
right?)—and only learned later that they
would come in the next day somewhat
aghast, believing everything about them
was wrong! Which it may have been, but
still.

Point being, not everything in DON'T
can be adhered to 100% of the time.
(Especially when you're new to New
York City, sometimes making it through
the day is a feat in itself—financially and
psychologically.) But breaking bad habits, which are generally bad habits from
omission, must be addressed or your

days here will be numbered. Do trust me.

And on that note... thank you. For reading DON'T, of course. I sincerely hope that you take these lessons in good humor, and don't think less of your well-meaning author. I also hope that you enjoy NYC with character; there's truly no other place in the world like it.

To Topher: Your dedication to things you want to do is impressive, and I'm very, very thankful you wanted to do DON'T. You're a bright light at PUBLIC.

To Nic: Just genius. Your talents have raised our company IQ by measures.

To Viia (editor): We adore your gift with language and your willingness to work within our confines. New York City would be a better place if you were here...

To Nathan (content developer): Totally appreciated, sir. Let's do another one.

To our PUBLIC family—Ryan, Erin and Tara: Your individual, and distinct, talents make us incredibly strong. Thank you for your continued efforts and unwavering loyalty.

To Steven and Francine Porter and to the "Bobcats"—a group of men living in this era but belonging entirely to another: Thank you for your teeming eccentricities, gentlemen, for indeed, they forever embody the ideals of DON'T. This may come as a surprise, but it is your exceptional quality as human beings that has become my adamantine source of inspiration.

Eric Larsen—"The Eccentric"
Ford Koles—"The Churlish Dandy"
Andy Lee—"Manscaped Sweetheart"
Scott Fassbach—"The Contrarian"
Matthew Carnahan —"Carnage, The Pugilist"

—Marco Larsen

THE BOBCATS: THE ECCENTRIC, MANSCAPED SWEETHEART

THE CHURLISH DANDY, THE CONTRARIAN AND CARNAGE,
THE PUGILIST

For my special wife, Sarah
(who deals with me)

COLOPHON

COPYRIGHTED BY PUBLIC
MARCO LARSEN 2009

www.publicnewyorkcity.com

This book was designed at vosbrenner by
Nele Vos and Michael Brenner

The typeface is DTL Fleischmann digitized from the
original by Erhard Kaiser in 1992